WE SAVE BITS OF STRING

WE SAVE BITS OF STRING

BETTY BIRCH

You can recognise us. We always clear our plates, we make do and mend, and we save bits of string. *Anon*

The true story of a working class girl growing up in the 1930s and 40s in a boot and shoe town in Northamptonshire

ST CHRISTOPHER PRESS
LONDON

2011

ISBN 978-0-9545721-2-9

This edition first published in 2011
by the St Christopher Press
16 Blake Gardens, Fulham, London SW6 4QB
www.stchristopherpress.com
admin@stchristopherpress.com

A CIP catalogue record for this title
is available from the British Library

Cover design by Chris Jepson

Printed in Great Britain by Blissetts

The photograph on the front cover is of the author, aged 4, wearing her
grandma's glasses and pretending to darn a sock

PREFACE

THIS MEMOIR covers the 18½ years during which I lived in Rothwell, Northamptonshire – from my birth in 1930 to my departure for Bristol University in 1948. My approach is thematic rather than chronological, so I sometimes dig into the pre-1930 past or forge ahead into the post-1948 future – but the heart of the matter is those years of the great depression, the second world war and the post-war austerity period and life as it was lived by my family and my community at that time.

I have written primarily for members of my own family, some of whom still live in Northamptonshire, but the Rothwell, Kettering and Desborough that they know today are dramatically different from the ones I knew as a youngster, and the life style of my little great-niece and great-nephews in Desborough is totally different from the one I knew at their age.

Items of ordinary household equipment familiar to my generation – the flat iron, the dolly stick, the gas copper, the backing bucket, the black-lead brush – have disappeared or become museum pieces, and foods familiar to me and my generation – faggots, chitterlings, water-glass eggs, Ro'well Fair tarts – are as alien to them as pizza or chicken tikka masala would have been to me at their age.

But some things endure. We had love and laughter and fun -- and so have they – and the warmth and security of a close and loving family is as vital to them as it has always been to me.

To my parents, Marion Ruth and Walter Andrew, this book is dedicated with love and gratitude

Contents

Acknowledgements

This is my book, about the first 18½ years of my life, but several other people have made important contributions to it, and I thank them most sincerely for what they have done.

They are

> First and foremost, my husband Chris, without whose encouragement and practical assistance the work would never have been completed. He has transcribed my almost illegible handwriting into readable typescript, helped with research, edited the text and made the necessary arrangements for publication. He was also responsible for the mammoth task of compiling the index.
>
> My children Frank and Harriet, who read and checked the script and made helpful suggestions for its improvement and clarification.
>
> My beloved Auntie Rene (Mrs Irene Cullis), my cousins Ruth Howes and Norman and Anne Tilling, and my old friend Graham Palmer, on all of whose memories I called when my own failed.
>
> Chris Jepson for the cover design, with which I am delighted.
>
> Colin Maitland of the One Roof Press, who was responsible for the typography and design of the rest of the book and for seeing it to press.

Responsibility for any mistakes and inaccuracies is, of course, mine.

CHAPTER I
Rothwell in the 1930s

I WAS BORN on 2 March 1930 at 36 Littlewood Street in Rothwell, Northamptonshire. My birth was attended by the district nurse, Nurse Panton, Nurse, and my maternal grandmother, Grandma Kirby. Fathers were excluded in those days but my dad brought my mother a bunch of daffodils, the only time, my mother said, that he brought her flowers in their 58-year-long marriage.

My arrival, however, was not greeted with universal enthusiasm. My mother's cat and my five-and-a-half-year-old brother, Wally, both precipitately left home. The cat was never seen again. Wally had only gone as far as our Auntie Hilda's house, just across the road, declaring he was going to live there now. She eventually persuaded him to let her bring him back, and in time he accepted the new situation.

Rothwell in those days was a small town (population 5,oooish), heavily dependent on the boot and shoe trade. There were six or seven boot and shoe factories, small by modern standards, and in 1930 they were all on short time. It was the depth of the Great Depression. My father, my paternal grandfather, Grandpa Andrew, and my father's two brothers, Charles and Leonard, were all on the dole or on short time for most of my childhood. The situation only began to pick up when war became imminent.

Littlewood Street at that time was frontier territory, at the very north-eastern edge of Rothwell. The houses on the northern side – some built about the turn of the century – were backed by allotments and farm land. The people that side could keep a pig if they wanted to, as the pigsty could be far enough from human habitation to comply with the law. Some of them did. At the eastern end of the street, the road ended abruptly at a corrugated iron fence, and beyond it was farm land. There is now a huge housing estate there.

Our house was on the south side of Littlewood Street, on the corner of Ragsdale Street – a long steep hill that led down, again, to farm land. Our house was one of a set of four (nos 30, 32, 34 and 36) put up by a local builder, Mr Tebbut in 1926. My parents bought it – I think for £600 (there is no one to check with now) payable over 20 years. They moved in in 1926 with two-year-old Wally and May, one of my mother's younger sisters who was living with them at the time.

The four houses were arranged as two pairs of semi-detached; we were semi-detached from Mr and Mrs Chapman. Our house, being the corner one, had a very slightly wider garden than the others. The houses were, I think, solidly and honestly built but had been run up as cheaply as possible and with not a lot of thought given to the convenience of the people living in them.

There were three rooms on the ground floor. The front room, chilly and uninviting, was used only occasionally when a fire would be lit, but the room never got really warm. Behind the front room was the living-room, the heart of the home and scene of most of our indoor activities, collective or individual. On the outside wall was the fireplace: an old-fashioned iron one which needed black-leading two or three times a week to keep it respectable looking. Black-leading involved applying a liquid black-lead polish with a special brush and brushing hard to create a shine. Hard, hot and dirty work, but necessary.

Set into the wall beside the grate were two ovens; they never got really hot and could only be used for slow-cooking stuff like milk puddings or drying off crusts of bread to make rusks or breadcrumbs. We used the cooler of the two as an airing cupboard for underwear and socks and jumpers and such.

The fire was alight every day during the cooler and colder weather: my father used to light it before he went to work in the morning. The hob in front of the fire was used extensively for cooking. Pots of vegetables or soup or stew would be cooked there, and my mother used to fry our breakfasts in a iron frying pan held directly over the coals. Horribly dangerous, of course, but I do not remember her ever having an accident.

Two kettles, a big brown one and a smaller blue one, were kept in the hearth, and that is where our boiling water came from in winter. Alongside the fireplace was a floor-to-ceiling cupboard, divided horizontally into three sections. The lowest section was a toy cupboard; I had the bottom shelf, Wally the upper one. Above that were two deep drawers where tablecloths and such were stored, and above that again a cupboard where our everyday crockery, tea, sugar, salt, pepper and all manner of miscellaneous items were kept.

On the other side of the fireplace was a smallish, free-standing cupboard, which my father had made – he was a very skilful carpenter – and we kept gloves and scarves and handbags in it. On top of it stood our wireless. The first one we had was made by my father from a kit, and inside it were two very thick, heavy, square glass jars called 'accumulators'. Every so often they had to be taken to a shop in the town to be charged.

The wireless I remember best was a large, varnished wooden affair bought from the Co-op. The aerial was a very high cable stretched between the top of our house and the next one down Ragsdale Street. Apparently it was very vulnerable to lightning and, if we were down in the town and thunder threatened, someone had to run like the clappers to get home and unplug it.

At right angles to the fireplace wall was a window overlooking the back garden; alongside it was my mother's sewing-machine, then the door to the kitchen. The wall opposite the fireplace accommodated my father's bureau and the door leading to the hallway and stairs. The remaining wall was occupied by a piano, above which hung the Vienna striking wall clock, which is still in my possession.

The living-room also held two armchairs, one on each side of the fireplace, four straight-backed chairs tucked under the table and the table itself, where we ate our meals, did our homework, played our board and card games, cut out our sewing patterns, did our ironing on a special board custom-built by my father and, in fact, pursued any activity except cooking that required a flat, horizontal surface.

It was a pretty full room, and there wasn't much space to move about.

Our back door was in Ragsdale Street, facing east and opening straight into the kitchen, which was bone-chillingly cold in winter. There was an alcove containing a gas stove, and the kitchen table was usually pushed up against it except on Sundays and Wednesday or Thursday when my mother used the oven and the table had to be lifted out and placed in a position that made it difficult to get about in the kitchen. Most days my mother just used the gas rings on top of the stove for cooking, leaning awkwardly over the table to do so. We had a shilling-in-the-slot meter for gas in the space under the stairs and tried to feed it as little as possible.

There was an earthenware sink with a cold-water tap connected to the mains water supply and a hand pump that drew up rain water from a well. Many houses had a well at this time. My father, as I have said, was a good carpenter, and he had fixed a number of shelves and work surfaces in the kitchen. There was a decent-sized pantry off the kitchen; no fridge, of course, but a meat safe with a metal mesh door to protect the contents from flies.

Beyond the kitchen was an outdoor lavatory and, next to it, a workshop that we called 'the barn'. Here my father mended our shoes (I still have some of the lasts he used) and did all manner of repairs and other small jobs. Root vegetables were also stored in the barn in winter. Beyond the barn and lavatory was a corrugated-iron coal shed, which my father built. If you wanted to go to the lavatory or the barn or fetch in some coal, you had to go out of the back door and walk along an exposed concrete path – laid by my father – whatever the weather or time of day.

We hardly ever used the front door; it was permanently locked and bolted. The papers and post were delivered through its letter-box, and that was about the only purpose it served. There was a narrow passage way from the front door to the bottom of the stairs, also narrow and steep. We never talked about 'the hall' or 'hallway'; it was always referred to as 'the passage'. It was made even narrower by a collection of coats, jackets and such hanging from a row of pegs along one side.

Upstairs were three bedrooms. Nothing else. No bathroom.

There was quite a bit of house-building in Rothwell between the wars. Some houses went up in Rushton Road in the early '30s, one of them subsequently bought by May's husband when they married in 1933. There was also a big council estate, Westfield Place, built at about this time in the south-western corner of the town.

During the second world war employment picked up. My father worked every day and even worked overtime, and my mother earned a little here and there. They were naturally frugal people, and anyway there was nothing much to buy, so they were able to put some money aside.In 1946 they finished paying for the house – it was theirs – and they set about a house improvement programme. My father's skills did not extend to bricklaying or plumbing, and the work was done by Reg and Ernie Johnson, brothers who ran a small building firm, but the planning was done by my mother, who knew exactly what she wanted.

The back door was repositioned, so that it opened into the space by the lavatory and barn, which you could now reach under cover. A Raeburn coke-burning stove was installed, transforming the icy kitchen into a cosy little haven. The barn was built up a foot or so, and another bedroom built above it. And the smallest of the original three bedrooms became a properly equipped bathroom, the water being heated by the Raeburn.

Rothwell was a Co-op town, and we were a Co-op family. My paternal grandfather, Grandpa Andrew, was president of the Co-op for years. When he died in 1954, all the Co-op shops in the town closed for the afternoon of his funeral as a mark of respect. Mum was chair of the Co-op Women's Guild for years. Uncle Bill, Grandpa's older brother, ran the Co-op penny bank on a voluntary basis. We bought everything at the Co-op – meat, groceries, bread, coal, any clothes that were not made at home – everything but milk, which for some reason the Co-op did not provide until the end of the 30s.

Our Co-op number was 1158. It was, and still is, engraved upon the heart of every family member. When you were sent on an errand to the Co-op, they wrote your number and the amount of your purchase on a little pink slip which they gave to you. They kept a carbon copy. Woe betide anyone who forgot the number or lost the slip. The slips were carefully stored in an old cream cracker tin and twice a year, early in December and early in June, Dad totalled up all the amounts to make sure the Co-op had it right when they assessed our dividend payment.

This 'divi' was our share of the profit made by Rothwell Co-op after costs were met. It was usually a good payment, often as much as a shilling in the pound (5%), and was a godsend to working class families. Our December divi was used for Christmas, and the June one was saved for our annual August visit to my mother's family in the Forest of Dean, of which more anon.

There were two Co-op shoe factories in Rothwell, the Littlewood Street Avalon and the Fox Street Avalon, and there was a Co-op corset factory, the Desbeau, in Desborough, another small town about two miles from Rothwell.

There were other shops, of course, small independents, but we didn't use them very much, though I would sometimes be sent on a Sunday to Munton's, a little grocer-cum-off-licence – and therefore open during licensing hours on Sundays – to buy vinegar for the mint sauce. Vinegar was sold loose; you took your own bottle, and Mr Munton poured it in with a little measuring jug. Mr Munton also had a fish shop elsewhere in the town.

You could choose from four places of worship: Church of England, Congregational Chapel, Wesleyan Chapel or Salvation Army. No Catholics. I only ever knew of one Catholic family in Rothwell during my childhood, and they had to go to Kettering, five miles away, to go to church. We were a Congregational Chapel family. Mum had been brought up C of E, but Dad's family were Chapel, and Rothwell was his home territory, so Chapel we were.

My parents were both highly intelligent and talented but, being born into the working class at the beginning of the 20th century, they were not able to fulfil their potentials in the labour market. If they had been born into the middle class, my father might have been a mathematics teacher or accountant and my mother a hospital matron if not a doctor. Work was hard and physical, and long hours of it were needed to pay the mortgage, put food on the table and give their children a better start in life than they had had. Yet both of them found the time and energy to make valuable voluntary contributions to their community, in which they were known, liked and respected.

CHAPTER 2
My dad

MY DAD, Walter Andrew, was born on 11 February 1900. His parents, Alfred John Andrew and Sarah Murkitt, had been married the previous October when they were both 20 years old and Sarah was pregnant. A lot has been made in literature and sociology of Victorian attitudes to extra-marital sex, but in my experience it was always just a fact of life. When I started school at the council school in Rothwell, there were two little boys in my class who were illegitimate – something I realised much later. But no one ever bothered about it. The children had been absorbed into their mothers' birth families, and in both cases they were mainly brought up by their maternal grandparents. No one stigmatised them or told us not to play with them.

Later, during the war, when the young men of the town had been conscripted and young American airmen stationed near by, every so often there was a nine days' wonder when a young girl or a young wife whose husband was away fighting fell pregnant, but everybody soon calmed down, and the child would become part of the family and the community. That was life. That was what happened. We were pragmatic – it was the middle classes who did the shock-horror thing.

Grandpa Andrew was descended from agricultural labourers in the village of Thorpe Malsor, but he himself worked in a boot and shoe factory in Rothwell: Butlins – Butlins shoe factory, where my father later worked. Grandpa was a man of strong principles. I have already mentioned his co-op and chapel loyalties; he was a Labour Party man too. I don't know if he was a foundation member, but he was certainly involved from very early on.

I have his copy of *The Book of the Labour Party, its History, Growth, Policy and Leaders*, published in three volumes in 1925, with its dedication: "To the Labour Rank and File, whose loyalty, devotion and self-sacrifice built up the Labour Movement and gave their leaders the opportunity of service." That was Grandpa and the rest of the family. We were Labour to the marrow of our bones. I'm glad Grandpa never lived to see 'New Labour'.

He was also a teetotaller – honorary secretary of the Sons of Temperance, a friendly society based on total abstinence. Friendly societies of one sort or another were a feature of working class life in the late 19th and first half of the 20th centuries. The early craft trade unions of the 1860s and '70s had often been friendly societies too, which meant that a member's union dues, among other things, insured him (in those days always 'him') against sickness and unemployment. The new trade unions in the '80s and '90s, catered for the unskilled, and they could not afford this cover. Unskilled workers could not have paid the union dues that would have been needed, so separate friendly societies developed with various cultural or ideological bases. The Sons of Temperance, and I think most other friendly societies, provided cover against sickness but not unemployment.

The 1911 National Insurance Act provided a contributory system of insurance against illness and unemployment but the friendly societies continued to provide extra sickness cover for workers and medical cover for their families. This continued until the establishment of the Welfare State after the second world war.

My father's birth was followed quite quickly by those of three younger brothers: Charles, Leonard and Fred. I don't know their birth dates. Fred died in infancy. I didn't even know of his existence until Grandma casually mentioned him in conversation when I was a teenager. Charlie and Len both had rather sad lives. Charlie's wife Annie died miserably of cancer of the throat, through which he devotedly nursed her. Their first child died at birth, and Gordon, their surviving son, committed suicide in his late 20s. Charlie, who lived in Desborough Road, Rothwell, eventually retired from the boot and shoe trade and died in the early 1970s.

Len's wife, Mabel, was always delicate, their little daughter Julie died of TB meningitis at the age of five or six, and Mabel died soon afterwards. This was during the second world war, and Len was in the forces. After he was demobbed, he moved from Rothwell to Kettering and remarried. His second wife, another Mabel, died before he did.

My younger brother John and his wife Jenny were very, very good to Charlie after Gordon died, fetching him for Sunday lunch and doing little things around the house that a son or daughter might have done. At one time Jenny made him some curtains. After Len's second wife died, they were very good to him too.

My father was very much his father's son, but a gentler version. Grandpa could be dogmatic and didactic; Dad wasn't. He left school at 13, having achieved 'standard seven'. When elementary education became compulsory at the end of the 19th century, a set of 'standards' was established, achievements that a child was supposed to reach at various stages in his/her elementary education. Standard seven was the goal at 14, the official school-leaving age since 1900, but a child achieving standard seven before the age of 14 could leave school early.

The 'standards' system seems to have been a precursor of the later 11+ examinations and even later SATS and league tables. I am, and shall always be, profoundly grateful that my own teaching experience was mainly in the 1960s and '70s when, briefly, teachers and pupils were given a bit of latitude to develop and explore at their own pace and inspectors were not breathing down their necks every five minutes.

The huge classes of my parents' time were named for the standard the pupils in them were being prepared for. My grandparents' generation still talked about being in 'standard one' or 'standard two' etc. They also called the Gladstone Street School, which my father and his brothers, Wally, John and I and all our Rothwell cousins attended, the 'board school', although the school boards, elected by the ratepayers, were abolished in 1902, when borough and county councils became responsible for elementary schools. My generation always called them 'council schools'.

My dad joined his dad at Butlins shoe factory in Kettering Road and, except for a period at the end of the first world war as a conscript soldier and periods on the dole, spent his whole working life in the service of Butlins, which was taken over shortly before he retired in 1965 by Clarks of Street in Somerset. I don't think he resented his lowly status in the economic pyramid. The work was repetitive and monotonous but called for a measure of skill, and he enjoyed the camaraderie of the factory floor.

Like his father, he joined the National Union of Boot and Shoe Operatives, now subsumed into a much larger general union called Community, and remained a member throughout his working life. We proudly display on the walls of our house in Fulham twin certificates stating that: "in recognition of Fifty Years Continuous Membership of this Union Mr Alfred/Walter Andrew of the Kettering Branch was made an Honorary Life Member and presented with a Free Membership Card on 1st August 1951/1st June 1967".

The union was a bit slow in getting its act together: Grandpa retired in 1946; Dad in 1965. The "fifty years continuous membership" only makes sense if the union waived dues for its members in the forces in the Great War or Grandpa paid Dad's dues. I don't know which.

Dad was 18 in February 1918, received his call-up papers and was instructed to report to Aldershot. Fortunately he was a brass bandsman, of which more later, and his skill with the soprano cornet meant that he was kept behind in England when his contemporary raw recruits were rushed to the continent to defend Amiens from the last big German offensive. Had this not been so, this story might not have been written. But the army valued brass bands – they were good for morale – and a group of these young recruits was welded into a band and in the mean time trained as signalmen.

Dad liked that. He had the sort of mind that enjoyed the precision of all the business with flags. It was during this time that he met one of his two lifelong friends, Robert Horsman, an 18-year-old Salvation Army bandsman from Eastbourne, my 'Uncle Bob', as I learned to call him. The welding together of the military band and the signal training delayed their departure until the very end of the war, when they became part of the army of occupation. Dad never talked much about this time, which seems to have been fairly uneventful. He was stationed near Cologne, liked the Germans he met, learned to count in German, picked up a few other words and returned to England in 1920 with a little model of Cologne cathedral, which lived on the mantelpiece of my parents' bedroom throughout my childhood.

So, back to Butlins. Life for a factory worker was hard, but preferable to the insecurity of part time or the dole. Throughout my childhood, when Dad was in work, he and Mum got up at 6.30 every morning. They washed in cold water at the kitchen sink, she cut some bread and butter for his breakfast, made tea for them both and a big jug of cocoa. She also prepared a substantial mid-morning snack for him to take to work – no works canteens in those days – bread and home-made dripping sandwiches, a small home-made fruit pasty, and a thermos flask of cocoa.

Mid-morning the factory suspended work for a quarter of an hour. This was called the 'lunch break', and the snack my mother prepared was called 'lunch' – a cause of some confusion later. Meanwhile Dad cleared the grate, lit the fire, got the coal in, swallowed his breakfast, kissed Mum goodbye and set off on the mile-long walk to Butlins. It was downhill going there and not too bad if the weather was fine. At 7.30 every factory in the town sounded a buzzer. Any worker who arrived after the buzzer sounded was late and was docked a quarter of an hour's pay.

Five hours after the start of work, the buzzer sounded again, marking the beginning of the one-hour dinner break. The walk this time was unremittingly uphill and took a good 15 minutes. A quick wash at the kitchen sink and then dinner, which had to be out on the table as he arrived. Not just in our house. In every house where a factory hand was coming home for dinner, the meal had to be out, on the table, to be attacked the moment he/she was there, and it had to be a substantial meal after the long morning's work.

My father's lot at dinner time was, in fact, worse than most, as Littlewood Street and Butlins factory were at diagonally opposite corners of Rothwell, but worse off still were the girls who worked at the Desbeau corset factory in Desborough. Two dedicated double-decker buses picked them up in Rothwell in the morning and took them to the factory, then picked them up at the factory at 12.30 and brought them back to Rothwell for dinner. Half an hour or so later they were picked up and taken to Desborough to start work again at 1.30.

The buses had two or three pick-up and set-down points in Rothwell, but the girls didn't wait for the stops. They crowded onto the bus platforms and jumped off the moving bus at the place nearest home. They were mostly girls in their middle or late teens. They would hit the road running and run all the way home, gobble up the dinners that their mothers would have put out ready for them and then run to the pick-up point.

There were two Desbeau girls in Ragsdale Street. Dad would usually have sat down to his dinner when we heard the clatter of running feet as Enid and Mary came home, and before he left for the afternoon shift, having got in the coal and made up the fire, they would be off again, running. Heaven knows what it did to their digestive systems.

The relentless factory buzzers sounded again at 1.30, and there was no afternoon break. They worked through until the buzzers released them at five o'clock. Saturday was a half-day; the five-day week didn't come in until after the war.

You might think that after a nine-and-a-half-hour working day standing at a machine plus four mile-long walks, a restful evening with newspaper or wireless would be called for – but you would be wrong. There was always something, usually something involving energy expenditure. After high tea, Dad would be off to the allotment, or into the garden or the barn, or to band practice or his Friendly Society round. It was really only on Sundays that there was any let-up – unless of course it was a spell of short time or dole, in which case there was too much let-up.

There was a fair-sized garden at Littlewood Street, and it was mostly given over to vegetables. We had a small lawn with a garden bench and a flower bed border, and Dad had built a trellised fence between the pretty bits and the vegetable area and trained a rambler rose up the trellis. He also built a trellised arch over the back gate and trained a climbing rose over that too. When Dad and Mum moved into their new home in 1926, someone (I don't know who) bought them a bunch of roses, and Dad planted a cutting from them from which the roses of the arch grew. When my husband, Chris, and the children and I moved into our house in Fulham, Dad took another cutting from the same rose bush and planted it in our garden, where it flourishes still, more than 40 years on.

We shared an allotment with Grandpa. There were several sorts of allotment round the edge of Rothwell, occupying quite a lot of land. Our set of allotments was administered by a firm called Kaybirds, who collected rents and enforced certain standards – you were not allowed to let your plot go to rack and ruin. Grandpa had the half nearest to the dirt track that ran down the allotment field. There was a shared hut at the half-way mark, and the other half was ours, but Dad and Grandpa often worked together on one half or the other.

We were pretty well self-sufficient in vegetables. Give or take an occasional tin of peas, Mum never bought vegetables, nor did most of the other housewives in Rothwell. Root vegetables were lifted in the autumn and stored in the barn for the winter, and the various brassicas were cut as needed in winter. Summer brought welcome broad beans, stick beans (always called 'kidney beans' in Rothwell) and peas. We had two or three rows of peas every year, though they were reckoned to be an extravagant crop, giving a small yield for the ground occupied. For the same reason, spinach was eschewed, and strawberries.

Wealthier members of our community sometimes had gardens large enough to accommodate a strawberry bed. Auntie May and Uncle Irvie had strawberries in their garden. We had a row of raspberry canes in the garden at home, and on late summer Sunday mornings after Sunday school, I would be sent out to pick raspberries for dinner. We also grew rhubarb and gooseberries to make puddings and preserves.

When the factory was on short time, I, as a small pre-school child, would sometimes go with Dad to 'help' on the allotment. He would give me a small fork and trowel to dig with and would pull up a young carrot and wash it in the water butt for me to eat as a snack. I enjoyed that, and I enjoyed having a ride in the wheelbarrow to and from the allotment. On summer and autumn Saturday afternoons we would often all go to pick peas or beans or gooseberries. Usually there were other families there as well, and other children to play with.

During the second world war allotments became enormously important but, of course, Dad and Grandpa had less time to spare as the factories were working all out, and Dad was an air raid warden.

One night a week my father went to band practice. Brass bands were enormously important in working class cultural life in the late 19th and first half of the 20th centuries. Our little town supported three flourishing brass bands in my childhood. My father played the soprano cornet in the Mission Band, which was attached to the Congregational Chapel. They played in public at various chapel events and at various outdoor locations around the town on Easter Sunday and Boxing Day and one or two other occasions. Sometimes they were asked to play at an event in one of the neighbouring villages and, if there was room in the coach transporting them, we and other children and wives might go too and take a picnic.

Once a year, in late winter or early spring, there was a Band Tea on a Friday after work. It was held in one of the chapel assembly rooms, and my mother and other bandsmen's wives (there were no bandswomen) would be prodigiously busy for a day or two beforehand preparing jellies and trifles and cakes, and on the Friday afternoon they would go to the assembly room and set out the trestle tables for a sit-down high tea. There would be ham and tongue which had been ready sliced by the co-op butcher, bread and butter to be cut, pickles and stuff and, of course, the sweet things.

I think the tea was held at such an inclement time of year because no one had fridges and most of the food items were perishable. After school that day, I and other children of bandsmen would go straight to the chapel, there to be washed and tidied up and put into our party frocks by our mothers. After tea the tables were cleared, folded up and put away. The band played, and there were dances and games. Washing up went on in shifts behind the scenes.

A week or so before or after the Band Tea, a Choir Tea was held for members of the chapel choir and their spouses and offspring. My second cousin Josie got to go to that one as her mum was in the choir.

Besides the Mission Band, there was the Town Band, aka the Albion Band, which played on civic occasions, and the Salvation Army Band: easily the most up-front and visible of the three. Every Sunday morning and on one weekday evening the Salvation Army Band would play hymns at various points around the town and would be accompanied by their choir who were called the Songsters. Their officer would say a prayer and exhort anyone standing about to join them. Their congregation, I'm afraid, usually consisted of curious children and a few dogs. There were nearly always dogs about our street, and we knew most of them by name.

Above our basic level, though, brass bands were quite big business. A number of industrial enterprises had their own bands, in which they took great pride. I remember Black Dyke Mills Band, which my father favoured, and Munn and Feltons Band, attached to the boot and shoe factory of the same name in Kettering, our neighbouring market town. Munn and Feltons would send their talent spotters round when the smaller local bands were performing, and a promising player would be offered work at Munn and Feltons factory and a place in the band. Band practice with a full-time bandmaster would be part of the working day.

These big, almost professional bands were very competitive. There was a National Band Contest every year, the finals being held at Crystal Palace in London before it burned down in 1936. After that they took place in various venues about the capital. There was great excitement and speculation beforehand, and Dad and his great friend and co-bandsman George Boyce used to try to scrape together enough for the fare and go up to London for the big day. They didn't always make it; sometimes they had to be content with listening to it on the wireless.

Friday night was 'club night', the club being the Sons of Temperance. I am not sure when my father took over the secretaryship of the Rothwell branch from Grandpa, but it was either before I was born or when I was very young. We had a brass plate alongside our front door engraved 'Sons of Temperance Friendly and Approved Society Hon. Secretary' or something like that. The brass plate was polished with Brasso every week and, when I was seven or eight, this became one of my Saturday morning jobs.

Friday night was also bath night. When Dad got home, after he had had his tea, he fetched in the tin bath and the gas copper from the barn where they were stored during the week and put them in the kitchen. Either Mum or Dad would fill the copper with perhaps a dozen jugs of water from the tap over the sink, light the gas and let the water heat up. The heat from the copper warmed the kitchen up a bit, but a bath in the winter was still a chilly experience. When we were small, we had a nightly bath in a much smaller tin tub in front of the living room fire, using water boiled up in a big saucepan on the hob. That was much nicer.

But eventually we had to use the bigger bath that had been brought into the kitchen. Water would be run from the tap near the bottom of the copper into the bath and a jug or so of cold water from the sink added until the temperature was right. As the bath water cooled down, some of it would be ladled back into the copper to re-heat for the next person. I, as the youngest, had the first bath and was therefore the only one to start with perfectly clean water. Wally followed, then Mum, then Dad when he got back from his round.

It was a long drawn out, laborious and not very enjoyable experience, and on Saturday morning the bathwater had to be ladled out and emptied down the sink and the bath and copper returned to the barn.

No wonder one of Mum's priorities when alterations were made to the house after the war was the building of a proper bathroom with hot water on tap and a plug hole to drain the water away. I expect that a similar ritual took place in most working class homes in Rothwell and, despite the labour involved, most of my contemporaries were clean and sweet-smelling.

But back to my father's Friday nights. After the business with the bath and copper, he washed, shaved and changed into his good suit and set off on his rounds, taking notebooks and cash from the locked drawer in his bureau in the living room. I don't know how many people were on his books, but the round took three hours or so. There were subscriptions to collect and payments to be made to those who were sick or unable to work, and everything was noted down. Later, before the next Friday, often late in the evening, information from the notebook was transferred to the official record books.

My father's books were meticulously kept and were models of neatness. Twice a year his friend George Boyce checked them, and I think every year they were sent to Nottingham to be audited. I don't think anyone ever found a mistake.

I find it very moving that all over the country there were working men, like my father, and some women, for whom there were never enough hours in the day or shillings in the pay packet, who gave up their time and scrupulously handled considerable sums of money running Friendly Societies, trade union branches, Labour Party branches, Communist Party branches and all the other organisations that helped their fellow workers survive in the harsh economic climate of the early 20th century.

My father was not the kind of militant, evangelical teetotaller that Grandpa Andrew was. He never went inside a pub, and we never had alcohol at home. He would have described himself in those days as a total abstainer. Much later in his life, when he and Mum and Wally moved to London to live near us, we led him astray and he got to enjoy a glass of sherry or cider at our house. One year, near the end of his life, I said to Mum: "I can't think what to buy Dad for his birthday. Any ideas?," and she said: "Well, it sounds funny, but I think he might like it if you got him a nice bottle of sherry". So I did, and he did. A bottle of Harvey's Bristol Cream proved to be just the ticket.

What else? I have said that my father was skilful carpenter. In his youth he made complicated fretwork picture frames. I can remember them when I was a young child, but I don't know what happened to them. He made a free-standing cupboard to keep his clothes in. I think my son Frank has it now. One Christmas, I think 1933 or 1934, when work was very scarce and money very short, he made me a doll's bed from bits and pieces of wood. It was a beautiful piece of work, accurately proportioned and meticulously finished. My mother, a skilled needlewoman, made a mattress, pillows, pillow-cases, sheets, a blanket and an eiderdown to measure. The whole thing cost almost nothing in cash, but hours of skilled work, patience and love went into it. It would not have been out of place in the toy department of Harrods.

A dozen or so years on, there was a bit more cash, but it was the end of the war and the period of post-war austerity, so no toys for sale. Dad made a railway engine for my little brother John. It was a solid wooden affair, painted red and black with wheels that turned, sturdy enough for a small boy to sit on and propel with his feet. John and his friends had hours of fun with it.

When Dad moved to London, he used to poke about in skips and round the market for odd bits of wood. He used some of them to make me a neat little spice rack to exactly fit a space on my kitchen wall, and he made my daughter Harriet a little shelf unit for her bedroom.

I think my father's carpentry skills were learned from his paternal grandfather. I have a little wooden stool which great-grandfather Andrew made for my father when he was a toddler. Over 100 years old now, it is still practical and serviceable.

My father was very numerate and enjoyed exercising his mathematical skills. We used to take *Reynolds News*, the national co-op Sunday newspaper, which every week carried a mathematical poser. My father and I used to pit our wits against each other to see who could solve it first. When I was preparing for School Certificate (fore-runner of O levels and GCSE), he would ask me to explain the maths I was doing and, though he had only been taught the most elementary arithmetic at school, he took to geometry and algebra like a duck to water.

It was part of the same mind set, I suppose, that he enjoyed jigsaw puzzles. When I was little, if he had been left to put me to bed, I would get him started on a puzzle a bit before bedtime. When he was hooked, I would slip off to my own devices, and Mum would come home to find him still puzzling and me still up and playing. Then we both got into trouble.

I could probably go on, but you can see that I thought a lot of my dad.

CHAPTER 3
My mother and her father and his three wives

MY MOTHER, Marion Ruth Kirby, was born on 11 July 1902. She was her father's eighth child and her mother's second. It's a bit difficult to make an accurate chronological account of Grandpa Kirby's early life, but the main facts are clear. He was born on 11 January 1862 at Langtoft in Lincolnshire into an agricultural family. His parents, Mark and Eliza, were both illiterate. They signed their marriage certificate in June 1858 "The mark X of Mark Kirby" and "The mark X of Eliza Bell".

When Grandfather was born, his mother registered his birth and again signed the register with an X. Yet Grandfather, as I and others remember him, was highly literate and educated well above the basic level. So where did he go to school? Or how else did he come by an education? And who paid? This was before the days of free compulsory education.

The next piece of documentary evidence I have for him is a marriage certificate dated 22 November 1886 when he married Mary Jane Blatherwick, aged 18, at Bracebridge in Lincolnshire. The occupation of both Grandfather and his father-in-law is given as 'Market Gardener'; they might have been master and man or work colleagues.

Poor little Mary Jane lived for less than two years after her wedding, dying of meningitis in August 1888. The young widower is described as a butler on the death certificate. He had previously been a footman at Launde Abbey, a rather grand country house in Leicestershire, parts of which date back to the 1550s. I have a framed photograph of him in his footman's finery, and a splendid figure he is.

He is still described as a butler on his next marriage certificate in February 1891, when he married Lucy Partridge at LoddingtonParish Church in Leicestershire. Both Henry and Lucy give Launde Abbey as their 'residence at the time of marriage', but there is a blank in the space for Lucy's occupation. Lucy was the elder sister, by nine years, of my maternal grandmother, Harriet Partridge.

Henry and Lucy left Launde Abbey soon after their wedding, for their daughter Lucy Annie was born some ten weeks later at the Cock Inn in Blakeney, Gloucestershire. Grandfather's occupation is given as 'Innkeeper', though whether he was owner, tenant or employee I do not know. In the 1891 census, he is described as 'Publican'. Auntie Rene, my mother's one surviving sibling, thinks he was pretty certainly the licensee but not the owner. But, whatever his status, the move to Blakeney seems precipitate and a bit odd.

Three more daughters rapidly followed: Harriet Jane in February 1893, Emma Elizabeth in November 1894, and Agnes Gertrude in February 1896, ie four children in slightly less than five years.

Hilda Emily was born on 10 April 1897, only 14 months after Agnes Gertrude, and by then the family had moved again – to Coleford on the western edge of the Forest of Dean (Blakeney is on the eastern edge). Lucy had been born in Coleford, and her widowed mother and possibly some siblings still lived there. Maybe Lucy felt the need for a bit of help from her birth family with all those children. On Hilda's birth certificate, Grandfather Henry Kirby's occupation is given as 'Butcher Master' and the place of birth as 'St John's Street, Coleford', where Grandfather now ran a butcher's shop, Again, I don't know if he owned or rented or was an employee at the shop, though the 'Master' in his job description suggests ownership.

One more child, their first son, Harry Mark, was born to Henry and Lucy on 10 February 1899. Before little Mark was a year old, Lucy was dead; she died on 1 December 1899. Auntie Rene says in her memoir that Lucy died in childbirth, but my mother thought she died of food poisoning from eating watercress from a polluted stream. Maybe I shall find out one day.

Meanwhile Harriet, my grandmother, had grown up and gone into domestic service, first at one of the more well-to-do houses in Coleford, and then farther afield. I don't know the details but I do know that by the end of this time she was employed as a cook, and in later life could tell wonderful stories of the dishes she cooked and the dinner parties at which they were consumed.

I think her last post must have been in or near Eastbourne, for she was courted by and married a young coachman, Bernard Tedham, from Eastbourne. Harriet and Bernard were married at St John's Church, Coleford, on 14 July 1896. She was 24, he was 27. It was a double wedding. Harriet's 19-year-old sister Gertie, was married at the same time to Thomas Edward Jones, a 21-year-old miner.

Bernard Tedham owned a horse and carriage, with which he ran a taxi service. Eastbourne was a busy resort, and there was plenty of demand for his services. My Grandma Harriet was occasionally employed to cook for dinner parties. Life was good but the good times didn't last. Just a year after the wedding, Bernard suffered a terrible accident involving his own runaway horse and carriage. He fell from the carriage and fractured his skull and a leg and died two days later in hospital, leaving Grandma a widow. About four months earlier, her sister Gertie had died in childbirth.

My mother told me that there was a photograph of Bernard Tedham on display in her childhood home, and she asked her mother who he was. Grandma told her the story, and my mother looked at the photograph and then asked "What shall I call him?". Grandma said "You can call him Uncle Bernard".

But back to Eastbourne. Grandma was offered a post with a Mr and Mrs Searle, for whom she had previously worked. Mrs Searle's health was not good, so the couple were planning to travel in France and Switzerland for several months. Grandma went with them as a nurse companion and spent a very pleasant time travelling and living in good hotels; she had many tales to tell of her foreign adventures.

When the Searles returned to England, they settled in the Isle of

Wight, and Grandma stayed with them, enjoying a quite luxurious life style. But it was not to last. Grandma's mother, my great-grandmother Partridge, appealed to her to come home to Coleford and help care for Lucy's six motherless children. What a daunting decision to have to take: five little girls and a baby boy, all under the age of eight! But she took it, resigned her comfortable position and took on what must have been an incredibly difficult task – and she took on Henry too.

Their first child, Winifred Nellie, was born in February 1901. She was born prematurely, weighing about two pounds, and everyone predicted that Grandma would never manage to rear her – but rear her she did, though for her first few years Nellie was a fragile and delicate little creature. My mother, Ruth, born some 16 months after Nellie, was altogether more robust.

By the time Ruth was born, 11 July 1902, Grandfather's business had failed. He rented out the shop, though the family continued for several years to occupy the house behind and above it. Grandpa went back into service as butler to Sir Charles Palmer of Newland, just down the road from Coleford, but a live-in job of course though he was able to visit his family on his days off. So there was Harriet with a new baby, an extremely delicate 16-month-old, and six other children, the oldest aged 11. Heaven knows how she coped, but cope she did – brilliantly.

She bore Henry two more children in the St John Street house: John William in June 1905 and Nora May in May 1907. I have a framed photograph of the family taken probably in the early summer of 1906. Grandma and Grandpa are seated, with baby John on his mother's lap. The five older girls stand behind and alongside. Seven-year-old Mark stands beside his father. Nellie and Ruth are seated in front. I find it absolutely awesome that, apart from Grandpa's suit and possibly Mark's little jacket, every stitch of clothing worn by everybody in the photo was made by Grandma on her hand-operated sewing-machine and kept in pristine condition by Grandma with an old fashioned wash-tub and flat-iron.

The year 1907 seems to have been an eventful one. Not only was May born, but Grandpa and Grandma were able at last to get married. They had been prevented hitherto by Canon Law. Both Church and State forbade marriage between a widower and his dead wife's sister, but the Deceased Wife's Sister's Marriage Act 1907 removed this prohibition, so they went off to Monmouth Register Office and were married on 7 November 1907.

Soon after their marriage the family moved from St John Street to 8 Albert Road, a house built by Grandma's father, John Partridge and where his widow had brought up their family. She, Grandma's mother, Elizabeth Partridge, continued to live there with the family until her death in 1916. She was about 83 when she died and could, according to my mother, remember 'the hungry '40s'. My mother remembers her granny being one of the first old age pensioners. In 1908 the Old Age Pensions Act was passsed, authorising the payment of five shillings a week to men and women over 70 provided they were not receiving poor relief and were earning less than 12 shillings a week.

Mum remembers her granny, to whom she was devoted, coming home with her first pension payment, pleased and proud that she had been one of the very few claimants able to sign her name; most had 'made their mark'.

Somewhen about this time, Grandpa left Newland to become butler to a Mr Jenner-Fust, the squire of Hill, a village between Berkeley and Thornbury. I presume it was a larger establishment than the Newland one and therefore the post was better paid. But it was farther away, so Grandpa couldn't visit his family as often.

Two more children were born at Albert Road: Thomas Patrick in March 1911 and Irene Mary in August 1914, 11 days after the outbreak of the first world war.

Because of the pressures at home when she was a toddler, Mum was allowed to go to school before she was three. She was too little to join in proper lessons and used to sit by the schoolroom fire and do what was called 'fraying'. This meant pulling strands from a piece of woven material to make a soft bundle of loose threads. The bigger girls who finished their school work quickly also did 'fraying' while waiting for their class mates to catch up. The results of the 'fraying' were sent to Gloucester and used as stuffing for cushions and pillows and such, and presumably the school received payment, which was used for extras.

Certainly the school, St John's Girls School in Coleford, seems to have been ahead of its time. Mum used to describe child care classes where they were shown how to bathe and dress a big baby doll, and she said that hot cocoa would be provided in winter for girls who lived too far away to get home for dinner.

Mum loved school. She loved reading and writing and learning poetry and drawing and painting. She was not so keen on arithmetic, but got by with it. She also loved the headmistress, Miss Voyce, and I think she was a bit of a favourite. When she left school, Miss Voyce gave Mum a little framed photograph of herself. It used to stand on the mantelpiece in our front room at Littlewood Street when I was a child. I don't know what happened to it afterwards.

Mum was very, very sad to leave school, but the big world was out there, and there was work to be done. Reluctantly she embarked upon it.

The Forest of Dean was coal-mining and forestry country. There wasn't much paid employment for girls apart from domestic work for the more prosperous households, or occasional shop work. Grandpa's girls went into service. There must have been some kind of grapevine whereby he learned of vacancies in large establishment or possibly vacancies were advertised in newspapers that he saw. A girl would be employed in the first instance as an under-maid in the kitchen or in the parlour or as an under-housemaid and might later be promoted to kitchen-maid, parlour-maid or housemaid or even to head housemaid. There was a rigid hierarchy of servants in wealthy households. The top jobs for women servants were cook or housekeeper, and for indoor male servants the top job was butler.

Of the Kirby girls, numbers one, two, three, four and six accepted their lot more or less philosophically. Numbers five and seven, Hilda and Ruth, my mother, hated it totally and unremittingly from first to last. Nellie and Ruth were found posts in the same household – Nellie as under-housemaid, Ruth as under-kitchen-maid – at the house of one Russell Thomas.

The house, Heneage Court, was near Berkeley, across the Bristol Channel from the Forest. Russell Thomas owned a soap factory in Bristol – Thomas's Matchless Cleanser was the product. My mother referred to her employers disrespectfully as 'The soapy Thomases', or 'Ma Thomas and Pa Thomas' or 'Him and Her'. Years later she wrote "There were five of us indoor staff: parlour-maid, cook, head house-maid, under-housemaid and myself. It seemed a lot to look after just two people."

There was also an assortment of gardeners, grooms and such – the outdoor staff. Mum's attitude has certainly rubbed off on me. I have always felt a bit uncomfortable employing someone to do any do-mestic work for me, and take pains to make it an equal, friendly rela-tionship. The Thomases had no such qualms, and my mother fretted and fumed and dug her heels in whenever she could. She refused to be suitably grateful when presented at Christmas with a length of calico to make herself a pair of knickers. She insisted in putting flow-ers in her black straw hat for the obligatory Sunday church-going. She would not wear a mop cap.

I think Grandma had insisted that Ruth and Nellie be found posts together, thinking her delicate elder daughter could do with her stronger sister's support, but I'm afraid poor Nellie must have often been embarrassed by her stroppy younger sister. At about the time (I think 1917) that Nellie and Ruth went into service, 20-year-old Hilda was making her escape.

The post Grandpa had found for Hilda was in Market Harborough, in south-eastern Leicestershire. I don't know what her job title was but her duties apparently included boiling potatoes. Market Harborough was a small, flourishing market town with developing light industry, including a factory called Symingtons, which made soups, custard powder, blancmange powder and such commodities.

There was a certain amount of working class social activity, including dances, cinema and such. I expect Hilda was forbidden to indulge on her weekly half-day off, but I am pretty certain she ignored the prohibition. Anyway, one morning a full-blown row blew up between Hilda and the lady of the house, culminating in Hilda's throwing a panful of hot potatoes at her mistress, telling her "you can boil your own bloody potatoes". And with that she stalked out of the house and sought refuge with the family of a young local woman she had met in town, perhaps at a dance. This young woman worked at Symingtons.

When I first heard this story, the row was presented as a piece of spontaneous combustion, but I don't believe it. I think clever Hilda set the whole thing up. She had a bolt hole to go to and the prospect of a job. I knew her well. She was not at all a confrontational woman, but she needed the row to make sure her ex-employer would not take her back and would not provide a reference for any other job in service. It was a consummate piece of boat-burning.

Predictably, Grandfather took time off from butlering to go to Market Harborough to sort things out. But the conflicting parties were adamant, and Grandfather retreated, defeated. Game, set and match to Hilda. Bravo! A year later, aged 21, she married a young socialist republican, Ernest Giles, my Uncle Ern, as he became, from Desborough, a small town just across the county border in Northamptonshire.

Meanwhile, back in Berkeley, my mother continued her servitude. She was paid £6 a year and had to buy her own print frocks, stockings and caps. I can't remember if she got a week or two weeks' holiday a year, but early August 1919 found her at home in her beloved Forest starting a much needed and anticipated holiday. Hilda and Ern were there too. In those days the Northamptonshire factories closed for a week at the beginning of August. All looked set for a lovely family holiday, but then a telegram arrived from the Thomases. Ellen, their cook, had been taken ill and my mother was to return at once. She cried and fumed but Grandma and Grandpa, who seems to have been there at the time, said of course she must go.

"No", said Hilda. "She is not going. She is to have her holiday, and then we will take her back with us and find her a job". And, amazingly, that is what happened. Another piece of boat-burning. The Thomases, to give them credit, didn't take it out on Nell. She stayed with them, eventually being promoted to head housemaid. She finally left to marry a Berkeley lad, Jack Elliot.

With the move to Desborough, Hilda had left her job at Symingtons and took a new one at a factory called Rigid Containers. They made shoe boxes for the at that time flourishing boot and shoe factories. My mother got a job there without difficulty and settled happily into her new life.

Hilda's rebellion proved to be a catalyst in the Kirby family. There appears to have been no question of the two younger girls going into service. May stayed at home for a year or two after leaving school, helping her mother in the house and with looking after the two younger children, before leaving at 17 or so to join her sisters in Desborough at Rigid Containers. Rene, the youngest, was able, under the terms of the 1902 Education Act, to take up a scholarship to the local grammar school, and later trained as a primary school teacher.

My mother was by no means intellectually challenged by her work at Rigid Containers for she was quick and deft and easily got through her work load. She enjoyed the company of the other girls of her own age and the freedom to choose her own clothes and to spend her time after work as she wanted. It was a far cry from cleaning the Thomases' saucepans and peeling their vegetables. Ern introduced her to socialist ideas and took her to Labour Party meetings, and her ideas about society began to fall into place.

One of the diversions available was the cinema – silent films still, of course – and it was in a cinema queue that she met my dad. They got chatting, got on, and soon were dating regularly – or, in the parlance of their own times, were 'courting'.

They got married on 6 August 1923. I have photographs of their wedding. They were a good-looking couple, and the wedding party was a sizeable one by the standards of the time. I counted 32 people in the group photograph. May and Rene were bridesmaids, as was Muriel Tomlins, daughter of the family's next-door neighbours and great friends at Albert Road.

At the end of the week, my parents returned to Northamptonshire and took up residence in Rothwell, where they rented two rooms at the home of Aunt Ginney, widow of a first cousin of Grandpa's. I never knew her; she died before I was born. The house was in Crispin Street and, ten months after the wedding, Wally was born there.

Two years later they moved to 36 Littlewood Street, the house I have already described. May moved in with them; they had more space now than Hilda and Ern – there was a spare room, and May's contribution to the housekeeping came in handy, as did her occasional help with baby sitting. Soon afterwards Hilda and Ern also moved to Littlewood Street, to no 42. Their eldest daughter, Mary, was born there in July 1928.

Theirs was the middle house of a row of five little two-up, two-down houses built at the end of the 19th century to house the growing contingent of boot and shoe operatives. Outside their back doors, the houses each had a narrow strip of garden. The gardens were divided by narrow brick-paved paths, but there were no fences or hedges. A pathway ran along the top of the gardens to a gateway in Ragsdale Street, right opposite our back gate.

When those houses were built, there was still quite a bit of 'out work' obtainable at the factories. There were certain processes that women could do at home, in their own time, between domestic chores, and at the end of each garden was a workshop, still commonly called 'the shop', where this work could be done. By the 1930s 'out work' had practically died out, and the 'shops' were used for storage, shoe mending, gardening equipment or whatever.

Once, when we were very small, Hilda's daughter Mary and I locked ourselves inside 'the shop'. I don't remember why; perhaps we had a secret piece of mischief in mind, or perhaps we just wanted to see if we could turn the key. We could, but we couldn't turn it back! Convinced that we would never see our parents again and would starve to death in 'the shop', we set up a loud wailing that soon had all the ladies in the yard, plus my mum and sundry others, congregated outside, assuring us that we would soon be rescued but clearly not sure how.

It must have been school holiday time because they were joined by Perce Woolstone, a young teacher at the council school, who had been born and brought up in the end house in the yard. He asked the ladies to be quiet and told Mary and me that he would get us out, but we must be sensible girls and calm down and do as we were told. He then said: "Now, can you get the key out of the door?". We could. "Put it on this paper, then," he said, pushing a stiff piece of paper through the gap under the door. We did as we were told, Perce unlocked the door, and we were reunited with our mothers.

I don't remember if we got a cuddle or a smack, probably both! I always had a great affection for Perce after that.

Having settled to marriage, motherhood and Littlewood Street, my mum found her spiritual home in the Labour Party, good, old-fashioned, socialist Labour, and the Co-operative movement. This is where she was comfortable.

Auntie Rene says in her memoir "Ruth was a radical socialist (I think that is what she was), determined not to kow tow to anybody as she considered herself as good as or better than anyone". As, of course, she was.

Party politics were a bit in abeyance during the war, but in 1945 the country, including Rothwell, was alive with political activity in the run-up to the July General Election: the first for ten years. Our sitting MP was a Tory, John Profumo, destined for future fame or infamy in the call girl / spy scandal of 1963. Our man was Gilbert Mitchison, a London lawyer, husband of the much more up-front and flamboyant Naomi, historical novelist, traveller and expert on Africa. She was by birth a member of the famous Haldane family. There was also an independent candidate, John Dempsey, a Rothwell man, standing as a Christian Socialist. He was a good man, but not in with a ghost of a chance.

We threw ourselves into the Labour campaign and did whatever needed doing. We addressed envelopes, noting with interest that there was a man called William Pitt and another called Edmund Burke actually living in Rothwell. Mum took me canvassing, but she was not really very good at it, spending ages notching up views and experiences with supporters or getting into prolonged, heated arguments with opponents and thus not canvassing many houses. With 'don't knows' she tended to get impatient; she couldn't understand why they didn't see sense at once.

In later years I learned from other mentors that the trick is to disengage yourself quickly and politely from out-and-out supporters and opponents alike and spend your time with the 'don't knows'. But that was not my mother's way; she was not the stuff of which canvassers are made. She was a smashing heckler, though. Between us we successfully disrupted a meeting at which Profumo was supported by Viscount Hinchingbrooke. More than half a century on, Mum and I still sometimes had a reminiscent giggle together about that meeting.

We rejoiced at the Labour landslide and welcomed the nationalisation programme and the National Health Service, but we became increasingly disenchanted with the Labour government's foreign policy and the Cold War. When I went up to Bristol University in 1948, I joined the Communist Party, and in a year or two my mum joined too.

As well as being involved in politics, my mother was a deeply committed member of the St John's Ambulance Brigade. She took a number of courses and passed a number of examinations. She was the unofficial first-aider in our street and neighbouring ones. People were always coming to our door with cuts and sprains and other minor injuries, and she would deal with them competently and tell them if they needed to visit a doctor or hospital.

Her medical knowledge and expertise served her own family well: she nursed her brother John successfully through rheumatic fever in the late 1920s and her sister Rene through tuberculosis just after the war. I think she attended the births of May's three children and certainly she attended those of Hilda's two younger daughters Margaret and Ann. Wally, my elder brother, was frequently ill, and she nursed him patiently and expertly.

During the war, she worked as a voluntary nursing assistant at Kettering General Hospital. I think she did three afternoons a week, and she loved it. The hospital was busy; sometimes casualties from bombing raids who could not be dealt with in their own cities would be brought there, and sometimes young American airmen would be brought in from some of the several large American Air Force bases in the area.

She was not fazed by any of the messy aspects of nursing; bedpans and dressings she could take in her stride. The only thing that really deeply upset her at the hospital was the awful racism displayed by the young white American airmen towards their black compatriots.

Figures and numbers were my father's thing; words were my mother's. She loved to read and bought cheap editions of classics from a book club, long defunct. We had a set of Arthur Mee's *Children's Encyclopedia* at home: ten volumes bound in blue hardback, which my parents had bought through some hire-purchase scheme. As soon as we could read competently and knew our alphabet, Mum showed us how to use the index at the end of volume 10 to look things up.

When I was at the High School, she enjoyed my English homework. She wasn't so keen on the grammatical analysing, which I rather liked, but she loved the poetry and creative writing. It was sometimes difficult to prevent her from taking over. She would read what I had written and make helpful suggestions, and I could tell she was itching to take a pen and have a go herself.

She enjoyed crosswords and word puzzles. We took a magazine called *John Bull*, which carried a weekly 'Bullets' competition, whose details I have forgotten but it involved a play on words. Mum was very pleased with herself when one of her entries won ten shillings: a considerable sum in those days. In 2000 The *Guardian* published a letter from her, saying "I am 98, and I finished today's *Guardian* Quick Crossword at 11.30am". She was still having a go every day at the *Guardian*'s Quick Crossword until about eight weeks before her death at the age of 101.

Whist-drives were an important feature of working class life in Rothwell; every organisation used them as fund raisers. The system was simple. You paid a few pence entry fee, and there were two or three prizes for the highest scorers. The prizes might be monetary – taken from the entry fees – or they might be items donated by members of the host organisation. Thus, if you were skillful or lucky or both, you might come home with half a crown or a pound of bacon or a bag of oranges – a bit of a lucky dip, really.

My mother was a whiz at whist and very competitive. She went to at least one whist-drive a week and, more often than not, came home with a prize. If she didn't, she blamed her partner for playing the wrong card at the wrong time. Later in life, when she came to live in Fulham, my son Frank as a teenager sometimes accompanied her to whist-drives and reported that the other old ladies were all desperately keen to have Mum as their partner, because she could remember every card that everybody had played.

Some of her talent must have been passed on, for I remember that Frank once won a pound of sausages.

I have already said that my mother was an expert needlewoman, a skill she learned from her own mother. Before she was married, Mum saved enough from her wages at Rigid Containers to buy a treadle sewing-machine on hire purchase. I have it still, getting on for a hundred years old now. She used it for all kinds of household making and mending and to make clothes for herself, for Wally when he was small and for me. Children's clothes were often made from the best parts of discarded adult garments, carefully unpicked and washed. When she made me a dress, if there was enough material left over, she would make a matching dress for one of my dolls.

As the machine was treadle-operated, I hadn't sufficient length and strength of leg to use it until I was 12 or so but, long before then, my mother taught me to plan, cut out and hand sew dolls' clothes, and I in turn became proficient, eventually making clothes for myself and my children.

My mother also taught me to knit. When I was about five, someone bought me a pair of child-size knitting needles and a ball of rainbow wool to make a doll's scarf. My mother cast on ten stitches and knitted a row or two to give me a firm start and then showed me what to do. I still remember the mantra: needle in, wool over, slip it through, knock it off – repeated patiently for each stitch until I had got the hang of it.

Again, making dolls' clothes, I learned to do various stitch patterns, to increase and decrease, cast on and cast off and all the other intricacies of knitting. Before I left the council school at the age of 11, I had successfully knitted a pair of gloves for myself, quite a complicated operation.

Also, while quite a young child, I learned to crochet, to smock and to darn, this last an essential in every household. In those days there were no synthetic yarns to reinforce woollen socks and stockings and, as everybody walked a lot more than they do now, there was always a pile of items waiting to be darned. These needle skills were imparted in those days by all conscientious mothers to their daughters, its being understood that, whatever else, they would be needed in adult life.

Again, I have gone on a bit, but you can tell that I thought a lot of my mum, too. I am proud of my parents and grateful for the values they gave me and the skills they taught me.

CHAPTER 4
The rest of my immediate family

MY BROTHER Wally (Walter Alfred Henry, born 7 June 1924) was a delicate child. Somewhere along the line in his childhood, he was diagnosed by a London specialist as having cystic fibrosis, but years later this was found not to be so. He had, in fact, some malfunctioning of his swallowing mechanism, so that from time to time bits of food got into his lungs and set up inflammation.

He was often ill as a child, and for quite a long time my mother had to take him regularly to Kettering General Hospital for treatment. If my father was working, this meant someone else had to look after me. This, in fact, meant either Auntie Hilda or Grandma Andrew. I was an equable child and quite happy with either arrangement. Auntie Hilda's first daughter Mary was nearly two years older than me but, once we grew out of babyhood, we were much the same size and played happily together.

There was not, of course, another child at Grandma's but there was the great excitement of Grandpa and Uncle Len coming home to dinner. Both used to make an enormous fuss of me, and Len always found time for a game. When they went back to work, he gave me a ride on his shoulders to the end of the road, then swung me down to ground level, they both gave me a kiss, and I ran back to Grandma, waiting at the gate.

When Wally was ten, he developed appendicitis with all manner of complications. He was in hospital for several weeks and needed lots of skilful nursing from my mother when he came home. He was too ill to take the scholarship examination, precursor of the 11+, which selected a small number of children from council schools to receive a grammar school education.

The examination was always held early in March and was taken by children whose 11th birthday fell in that school year. Wally was 11 in June 1935, so should have taken the examination the preceding March, and at first it looked as if he had missed his chance. But Mum made a huge fuss, and the upshot was that he was allowed to take the exam the following year. He was awarded a grammar school place and started at Kettering Grammar School in September 1936.

His grammar school career was not an unmitigated success. He enjoyed humanities and arts subjects but found scientific and mathematical subjects difficult and lacked the patience and application to get to grips with them. I still remember his throwing his schoolbooks around and raging and shouting when he couldn't get the hang of logarithms. He had a lot of trouble with Chaucer too. His health was still not good, and he missed quite a bit of schooling. The result was that he failed his School Certificate in the summer of 1941 and left school at 17 to work in an office in Kettering.

He was not particularly suited to or happy to be doing office work, and it lasted only about a year. He turned 18 in June 1942 and received his call-up papers. He was judged physically unfit for service in the armed forces, but had to accept direction 'to work of national importance'. He had sometimes helped out on a farm in his summer holidays as a schoolboy and had liked it – he always loved animals – and so he decided to go for farm work. But in winter it was too much for his delicate chest, and he had to do factory work instead.

When he was 23, he became very ill indeed and suffered brain damage. He made a partial recovery and was able to return to work. Uncle Irvie employed him in his family shoe factory and, with enormous tact and sensitivity, managed to keep him on an even keel. He needed a lot of care and support from the whole family, particularly from my mother, and at the end – he lived to be 75 – from Chris and me.

My little brother John was born in 1943, a bit of a surprise. I was 13 and Wally 19. While she was pregnant with John, my mother suffered a nasty accident. While tidying up the living room grate, she knelt on a splinter of coal on the hearth-rug and developed a serious infection in her knee, which required several days in hospital.

So, with the pregnancy and the knee, her war work at the hospital came to an end, and we all got ready for this new addition to our family. I was old enough and proficient enough to join in the orgy of knitting and sewing that in those days preceded the advent of a new baby, as opposed to the orgy of shopping that takes place these days.

Dad set about refurbishing a cot from Auntie May's attic, and we got a pram from someone, I don't remember whom. This was wartime, and new ones were not available, so Dad refurbished that too.

John was born at about 9 o'clock in the evening of 30 October 1943. Nurse Panton's successor and Grandma Kirby again attended the birth. Fathers were still not allowed in, but this time I was waiting with Dad. As soon as the baby had been tidied up, Grandma brought him out to us, and we both held him for a bit. Wally had been out but, when he came back, he looked at the baby and tentatively touched his cheek and hand but was too nervous to hold him.

So now we were five. We all bonded with this new arrival and loved him dearly. Wally was better than me at getting down to his level and playing with him on equal terms. When John was little, I think I was more like a third parent than a sister, but as adults we have an equal and close relationship.

John was not a well baby at first. He had a pyloric stenosis, which meant that he had to be bottle fed a specially thickened feed that took absolutely ages to administer. Fortunately there were several of us able to take turns giving him his bottle.

Auntie Rene and her daughter Ann joined our household a few weeks after John's birth, as Uncle Joe had been posted abroad and they had rented out their house in Gloucestershire, so we managed to get through those first difficult months without the need for surgical intervention, and the problem went away when he began to eat solid food.

John and I only lived consistently in the same house for the first five years of his life, as I went up to Bristol University in the autumn of 1948, a few weeks before his fifth birthday.

The two remaining members of our household in the 1930s were Joe and Peter. Joe was our cat, successor to the one who had so indignantly departed when I was born. There was at that time a sizeable piece of waste land in Ragsdale Street, a little way down from our back gate. It was a favourite playground for local children, and one Saturday morning Wally, aged about seven, was playing there with some friends when they heard some faint mewing. They searched around and found a tiny black kitten, apparently all alone.

Wally brought it home and begged to be allowed to keep it. Mum gave it a saucer of milk, and after dinner Dad and Wally went back to the waste ground to look around. They couldn't find a mother cat or any other members of a litter, so the kitten became our beloved Joe. I was told that at that time he could sit comfortably on the palm of Dad's hand, but when I first remember him he was a fully grown, magnificent young black tom, alert and predatory, strong limbed and with the most powerful jaws I have ever known on a cat. But he was gentle and mild-mannered in the house.

Joe was a mighty hunter. Apart from table scraps and an occasional saucer of milk, he kept himself in food. There was, of course, no specially manufactured cat food in those days. He sometimes brought us presents: mice and field voles mostly, but sometimes a young rabbit. He used to go hunting in the fields at the end of Littlewood Street. I think he was smart enough to realise that rabbits were particularly welcome for, while we thanked him politely for the mice and voles and disposed of them when he wasn't looking, Mum would paunch (ie remove the entrails) and skin a rabbit and put it in the stock pot.

Once he brought home a young chicken. Now there was a dilemma. Neighbours were glad to be rid of mice and rats, and the farmer was glad to be rid of the rabbits that nibbled at his crops, but to have your cat raid someone's chicken run was another thing altogether. Mum scolded the cat but, after he had slunk off, she plucked and drew the bird and put it in the pot. Well, what else would you do with a freshly killed chicken that had landed up in your kitchen?

Joe never caught another chicken or, at any rate, he knew better than to bring another one home.

Joe was a friend to all the family, but Wally was his favourite – his was always the preferred lap if Joe needed a bit of fuss. Once, when Wally was ill in bed, Dr Gibbons, our family doctor, called to see him. The doctor knew our house and family well. He let himself in without ceremony through the back door, said hello to Mum in the kitchen and then proceeded through the living room and up the stairs to Wally's bedroom.

Mum dried her hands and followed him up, and was mortified to find that Joe, who was not allowed upstairs, had somehow evaded her and was lying on the bed with a dead mouse he had brought us as a present. She made to shoo him away but "Let them be", said the wise doctor. "The boy is getting comfort and company from that cat". So only the mouse was removed and thereafter, if Wally was ill, Joe had visiting rights.

Peter was our rabbit. Dr Gibbons at one time did some kind of breeding experiment with rabbits and at the end of it dispensed rabbits to any of his patients who were willing to give them a home. We had two young bucks who came complete with a roomy hutch and a big bag of sawdust for bedding. We called them Peter and Paul.

They had not been with us long when one night they had a terrific fight, and one killed the other. The victor was Peter, who now had a nice big hutch all to himself. He was wary at first but was probably used to being handled a lot and responded to my stroking and playing with him, eventually becoming very tame. I used to take him out of his hutch and let him wander round the garden, taking care that he didn't eat anything that he shouldn't.

I also used to take him into the house in the evenings, and he liked to sit on my lap or to lie on the hearthrug in front of the fire in winter. He and Joe shared the warm hearth amicably and sometimes played together in the garden.

I think Joe regarded Peter as a sort of honorary cat, quite unlike the rabbits he hunted and killed in the farmers' fields. They were silver grey and moved like lightening. Well-fed Peter was black and white and moved at a comfortable lollop, and I suspect his scent was quite different. He may even have picked up some sort of human scent. He certainly picked up some feline behaviour traits. Joe, like all tom cats, was very territorial. If an alien cat ventured into our garden, he would see it off. Aggression was not usually needed. He would simply advance purposefully and menacingly, and the invader would slink off.

The same technique worked with most dogs he met in the street. I have seen him face down quite big dogs. Anyway, if Joe was not about and Peter was when a strange cat ventured into our territory, Peter would amble up to it in an enquiring "well, what can I do for you?" kind of way, and the cat would usually back off. I suppose they didn't meet that many assertive rabbits.

Like Joe, Peter cost practically nothing to keep. From time to time we bought a big bag of sawdust from a carpenter's workshop for bedding. He ate the coarser parts of brassicas, carrot and turnip tops, apple peel and cores and other discarded vegetable matter. When we went for a walk, we would take a paper bag and collect dandelions and sow thistles, his very favourite things – favourites, that is, apart from breakfast cereals.

We never ate breakfast cereals for breakfast but kept a packet of Grapenuts, a kind of bran cereal, and a packet of Force, an early variety of corn flakes, in the living-room cupboard and sometimes ate them as a pudding at dinner-time on Saturdays or as a bedtime snack. One day, opening a new packet of Grapenuts, Dad accidentally scattered a few on the floor, and Peter, who was about at the time, pounced upon them and wolfed them down. So sometimes we gave him a little saucer full of Grapenuts or Force as a special treat.

At the end of the day, both animals were put out: Peter into his hutch, which was in the covered area by the barn and was insulated with a thick rag rug in winter; Joe was let out to follow whatever courses of action there are for a tom cat left to his own devices at night.

Peter was with us for two or three years; then one morning he was found dead in his hutch. He had been perfectly all right the evening before. Mum and I cried, Wally blew his nose hard and Dad buried Peter at the end of the garden and I put flowers on his grave.

Joe survived well into the war years but began to get slower and less adventurous. Then one day he went out and just didn't come back. We searched and called, but he was never seen again.

I have never had, nor wanted to have, another rabbit. As an adult, I am not comfortable with the idea of putting a fellow creature in a cage. Cats are a different thing altogether. Alone of domesticated animals, they have freedom of choice and of movement and relate to human beings on their own terms. There has nearly always been a significant cat in my life.

Chapter 5
Relatives in Rothwell and the Forest

As you know, when I was born, there were three Kirby women in Littlewood Street, Rothwell: Ruth (Mum) and May at no 36 and Hilda at no 42. I don't remember May's living with us. She was married and moved into her new house a few weeks before my third birthday. She was a very pretty, lively girl who loved dancing, and it was on the dance floor that she met her husband-to-be, Frank Irving Groocock, whose family owned and ran one of the Rothwell shoe factories.

Uncle Irvie was one of the kindest, most considerate men you could ever wish to meet, always supportive and never condescending. He and May had three children, Tom, John and Elizabeth, born in 1933, 1935 and 1937. Uncle Irvie gave my mother a small regular sum of money to help May with the children, but the relationship seemed to be one of complete equality.

I spent a lot of time as a child with my Groocock cousins, eating tea on weekdays and dinner on Saturdays almost as often at their house as at my own.

In addition to Mary, whom I've already mentioned, Auntie Hilda produced two more cousins for me: in 1938, Margaret, a sweet fragile little girl who died of complications from rheumatic fever when she was about nine, and two or three years later, Ann, who still lives in Rothwell and whom I still see from time to time. Mary, Hilda's eldest daughter, died in November 2007. Chris, John and I went to Rothwell for her funeral.

I also had two first cousins on my father's side: Len's daughter Julie and Charlie's son, Gordon. I have written about them both in an earlier chapter.

Grandpa Andrew was the youngest of a family of 12, one girl and 11 boys. Grandma was the youngest of 13 – I don't know what the gender divide was for her family. The mind boggles at the thought of bringing up all those children on scanty, not very regular wages in the small inconvenient houses of the time.

I still have Great-grandma Murkitt's milk jug, a pretty, mass-produced mid-19th century pottery piece that I now use for large flower arrangements. In those days working class children were not given a cup of milk to drink – a scant spoonful in a cup of weak tea or cocoa was the norm. Nevertheless, the jug holds a good three pints. It had a lot of cups of tea to deal with.

I used to have her mixing bowl too, a vast iron-ware pottery one that I have used to make braised beef or chilli con carne for a party of 20 or so. I expect she made her everyday puddings in it. My daughter Harriet now has it.

The upshot of all this fecundity was that our little family had genes in common with a sizeable number of Rothwell's population. In Ragsdale Street, a little way down from our back gate and on the other side of the road lived one of Grandpa's older brothers, Uncle Arthur, a small kindly man who always moved at a brisk trot. His wife, Aunt Emma, was larger, slower, rather stately and a great knitter.

Opposite to Uncle Arthur and Aunt Emma lived their son Ernest and his wife Florence – Uncle Ernie and Aunt Flossie to us – with their sons Norman and Alan, a little older than Wally but great mates of his when they were children. Next door to them, in our direction, lived the Dimbleby's. Auntie Hilda Dimbleby was one of the daughters of Grandpa's only sister, Sarah Anne. She was Grandpa's parents' second child, so the Dimbleby children Mary and Cecil were quite grown up when we were children.

Next to the Dimbleby's and next to the fence at the bottom of our garden lived one of Uncle Arthur's and Aunt Emma's daughters, Nellie, married to Tom Kinch, an assistant at Messengers, the only posh grocer in Rothwell. Their daughter Josie was nearly a year older than me, and she and Mary and Heather Taylor, who lived a few minutes' walk away, were constant playmates in my childhood.

There were lots of other children around, who often joined us for games and walks. Josie was a very bossy little girl; she always decided what we would play and, if it was a role-playing game, she allocated the roles, usually assuming the star role herself: she was the teacher, or the shopkeeper, or the princess or whatever.

Once, it must have been in 1937, she decided we would play at Coronations, and she cast me as Queen Mary, the Queen Mother. For some reason I didn't understand, and still don't understand, my parents and any other adults to whom they told the story found this absolutely hilarious. And I don't mean just an amused smile reaction. This was real, bending double, thigh-smacking, rolling in the aisles stuff. I had forgotten about it until I began to write this memoir. Sadly, there is no one left now who can enlighten me.

Josie's mum, Aunt Nellie, like most other mums, made all of her daughter's clothes, and we were all very impressed that, when she made Josie a dress, she cut a narrow strip of matching fabric and machined round it to make a hair ribbon.

The Kinch family left Rothwell a year or so after the war started. They moved to Shropshire, where Tom had found a job to do with distributing animal feed to farmers. I think it might have been classed as work contributing to the war effort and therefore exempted him from national service. Josie and I exchanged occasional postcards for a while, but I'm afraid the correspondence petered out and we lost touch.

Every August in the 1930s (except one year which I will tell you about later) we went to Mum's family in the Forest of Dean. She had not lived there since she was 15 but, until she died at the age of 101, she always thought of the Forest as 'home'.

Dad came for one week only. The factory closed only for the first week in August. Even if it was on short time, he had to be around in case there was work available. He had his dinner at Grandma's but otherwise managed for himself.

Until I was six, we stayed at Albert Road, and we were quite a houseful. Grandpa was still working as a butler, of course, though he occasionally visited. Auntie Rene and Uncle Tom were still at home, and Uncle Mark whose marriage had foundered, was there with his two older daughters, Margaret and Doris. After his estranged wife died, the household was joined by his youngest daughter Nina, but that was after we stopped going to Albert Road.

We usually took a friend of Wally's with us, so it was quite a job to squeeze us all in, but Grandma managed it, as she managed everything, superbly.

Auntie Rene finished her teacher training and started teaching, I think about 1934, but she was on holiday in August, of course, and available for all kinds of games and outings and for helping Grandma. She was great fun and a wonderful young aunt to have and she came with an additional attraction. She was being courted by a lovely young man, Joe Cullis, the eldest son of a family who owned and ran a drapery and outfitters shop in Mile End, a small village about a mile from Coleford.

Uncle Joe, of course, was working during the week, but on Sundays he sometimes joined in our activities and fitted comfortably into our lives.

He was very accustomed to family life, having two younger brothers and two younger sisters.

Uncle Tom I adored, totally and unquestioningly. In photographs of our expeditions in the early '30s, I am usually being carried by Uncle Tom, either on his shoulders or in his arms.

Around the time of my sixth birthday, I began to pick up disturbing news from overheard adult conversations. "Our Tom", it seemed, "had got a young lady". I was incensed – a young lady indeed! What did he want with one of those when he had me? I think my attitude was discreetly passed on to the Coleford family.

When we went for our annual visit that summer, I met Ella, the young lady in question. She was pretty and lively and treated me as an equal. She told me how much she had looked forward to meeting me and how Tom missed me between visits and got lonely. She said that she and Tom were going to get married next year and I must be a bridesmaid, as I was already experienced in that role, and she would need my help. (I had already been a bridesmaid when Uncle Len married Auntie Mabel in June that year and was booked for Auntie Rene's and Uncle Joe's wedding on the last day of 1936.)

I was, of course, completely won over, and Ella and I became good friends and remained so until the end of her long life. The wedding took place on Easter Saturday 1937, so I was a bridesmaid three times in less than a year. The adults in my family joked that they could hire me out since I knew the ropes so well. I thought that was a jolly good idea. I liked being a bridesmaid: you got to wear a pretty frock, you were given a charming little trinket as a memento of the occasion and everybody made a fuss of you, especially if you were the smallest bridesmaid.

However, Tom and Ella were the end of the run; my parents' younger siblings were now all safely wed.

The year 1937 saw some changes in the family. Grandpa retired from butlering, and he and Grandma Kirby discovered they preferred to live apart, so he stayed at Albert Road with Uncle Mark and the girls, while Grandma went to live with Auntie Rene and Uncle Joe, who had bought a house called Fourways in Mile End near the shop. Thereafter, when we went to the Forest, we always stayed at Fourways, though we always visited Albert Road.

I didn't know Grandpa Kirby as well as my other three grandparents, seeing him only occasionally and briefly on our visits to Coleford. My mother had little to say about him, but Auntie Rene in her memoir recalls him as an affectionate and caring, though often absent, parent in her childhood.

While he and Grandma were trying to sort out their future after his retirement, he paid prolonged visits to some of his children. He spent two or three months with Auntie Emmie's family in Bristol. My cousin Norman, a young schoolboy at the time, had to share a single bed with Grandpa, while his three brothers shared a double bed in the same room. Norman has no affectionate memories of that time.

Grandpa also spent a few weeks in Rothwell. He was based at Auntie Hilda's. Mary was moved into a makeshift bed in her parents' room so that Grandpa could have her room, but he spent time at our house and at Auntie May's too. My cousin Tom, a very young child at the time, remembers playing Snap with him in the kitchen at the Rushton Road house.

I vividly remember his trying Marmite for the first time at our house. Mum warned him that it was strongly flavoured and should be used sparingly, but he took no notice, thinking perhaps that she was being stingy. He spread the Marmite as thickly as if it had been jam. Wally and I watched with great interest – we knew that Marmite was powerful stuff. Grandpa took one bite, and that was that. No more Marmite for him!

I thought that he took no particular interest in me, but I was clearly wrong. When things had settled down and he was living at Albert Road and we were staying at Mile End, probably in 1938, we called to see him. After we had exchanged news, he suddenly said to me: "Betty, I am going to give you the family Bible, because I know you will look after it" – and he did. We pushed it up to Mile End on the end of Ann's pram. I think my dad must have taken it back to Rothwell. It was, and is, huge and heavy.

Grandpa was right. I have looked after it in the condition in which it was handed to me. It certainly hadn't been well looked after before. Many pages are torn, and some are missing altogether. It is one of those vast, heavy, Victorian tomes with pictures, which Grandpa must have acquired himself – it had not been handed down to him.

He had entered on the relevant pages the births of all his children and some of his grandchildren, the marriages of some of his children – though not his own marriages – and one death, that of Lucy, his second wife.

His recording is rather careless – I found several mistakes. He had obviously relied on his memory. I am glad to have the Bible though and to know that he wanted me to have it. I don't think I ever saw him again. When my Groocock cousins and I were in Mile End in September 1939, we never visited Albert Road, and I did not return to Mile End until after Grandpa's death in February 1946.

I don't remember my mother's other two siblings, Nell and John, living at Albert Road. Nell, as I have already said, married Jack Elliot and they lived in Berkeley with their son Douglas, who was a couple of years younger than Wally. John married Win, a teacher, when I was a baby, and they had a son John, who was two years younger than me. Their daughter, Ruth, was born some 13 or 14 years later, the same kind of age gap as that between myself and my brother John. Uncle John and his family lived in Cinderford in the heart of the Forest. We used to see both families at some stage during the summer.

The Forest was fun and very different from Rothwell. There were far more wild places to explore and play in. Wild strawberries grew everywhere, the tiny, intensely flavoured, sweet 'wood strawberries'. Whenever you went out, you could pick a handful.

Sheep wandered everywhere. Foresters had the ancient right to let their sheep roam and graze at will. You would always be coming across them in twos or threes or sometimes quite big groups. They were always quite peaceful and amiable.

As well as the Forest itself, acres and acres of lovely woodland, there were large stretches of wild, open land known as 'means'. On the mean near Auntie Rene's house, someone kept a flock of geese, which were much more alarming than the sheep.

We often went on picnics. Grandma would pack the picnic fare in a clothes-basket covered with a clean tablecloth, carried between two of the adults or teenagers. Auntie Rene writes: "The picnic food never varied, a loaf of white bread, which was cut into thick slices and buttered, a tin of corned beef, tomatoes and hard-boiled eggs. Our desert was home-baked fruit cake".

There were lots of picnic sites, but there are three I particularly remember. We went to Severn Bridge at least once each summer. I am talking about the old railway bridge, the lowest crossing of the Severn until the road bridges were built well after the war. The old bridge has long gone, but it was an imposing sight in its day. The Severn was tidal and salty at that point. And dangerous. We were not allowed to paddle or play in it but, when the tide was out, there were piles of rocks covered in seaweed and rock pools to paddle in – and mud! Masses of lovely mud to make a mess with.

We went to the Severn Bridge by train. In the 1930s you could go nearly anywhere by train. This was way before Dr Beeching laid vandal's hands on what was a perfectly good and serviceable system. Sometimes Auntie Nell and Douglas came across the bridge from Berkeley to join us for the day.

Another favourite spot was Symonds Yat, a high rocky pile beside the river Wye with fantastic views in all directions. When Chris, Frank and I revisited it a year or so ago, it was well fenced in with footpaths you were meant to keep to but, when we picnicked there, it was wild and dangerous.

The other picnic site that sticks in my memory was Cannop pools, a mile or so from Mile End and so within walking distance of Fourways. It was a nice walk, across the mean to begin with, then through the Forest. It was downhill all the way there – some of the slopes were quite steep – and, of course, uphill all the way back. That was not quite so much fun.

There was a coal-mine at Cannop. Uncle Mark was a miner there, and so, briefly, had Uncle John been, until he suffered a terrible accident. He was crushed between two trucks loaded with coal. His physical recovery took a long time and skilful nursing by Grandma, but he never went down the pit again.

A lot of warm water was discharged from the Cannop pit and collected in a large open-air swimming-pool with a shallow paddling area for children. Wally and Uncle Joe's youngest brother and sister would swim, and I would paddle, and the grown ups sat and watched, no doubt glad of the rest after the walk.

When I was a child, they still used pit ponies at Cannop, and the Cannop ponies were reckoned to be lucky, in that they were stabled above ground. In a lot of pits, the poor little beasts never saw the light of day.

CHAPTER 6
A holiday in Eastbourne

WE DIDN'T GO to the Forest in the summer of 1937. As I have already said, certain re-arrangements were taking place in the Forest family, and we did something that Dad, particularly, had wanted to do for a long time. We went to stay with the Horsman family in Eastbourne.

Dad and Bob Horsman had not met since they were demobbed in 1920, but they had kept up a regular correspondence over the years. When Bob returned to Eastbourne from the army, he married Doris, his childhood sweetheart, and they started a family. Their son Wilf was about three years older than Wally, and their daughter Peggy was born about two years later.

They also had a little Cairn terrier called Chum, a real town dog, who only ever went out on a lead, firmly held by one of the family, quite unlike our Rothwell dogs who wandered about at will.

Bob and Doris did bed and breakfast lettings during the summer season, but I don't know what the financial arrangements were for our visit. We were there for one week only, the first week in August when the factories closed. It was the first time that the four of us had been together in a place that was totally unfamiliar, and my parents were a bit apprehensive about it.

I was made to repeat, over and over again, "My name is Betty Andrew. I am staying with Mr and Mrs Horsman at number 90 Sidney Road", a statement that must have been impressed upon me very firmly indeed, for it is still there in my memory, along with the Co-op divi number, the knitting mantra and one or two other miscellaneous items from early childhood. I was told that, if I ever got lost, I was to find a policeman and repeat the statement to him. He would then look after me until my parents came to find me, as they would surely do.

My parents knew their child. I *did* get lost. All of us except Wilf were on some expedition or other. I fell behind, probably to look at something, then set off at a quickened pace in what I thought was the right direction. No sign of anyone I knew; I must be lost. Right then: if you were lost, you had to find a policeman. While I was standing, looking around for a man in blue, a kindly looking middle-aged couple stopped and asked if I was all right. I explained that I needed to find a policeman and why.

The woman said she was pretty sure they had passed a policeman a minute or two ago. She would stay with me in case my family came back, and her husband would go and fetch the policeman, which he did in double-quick time, and I said my piece. The policeman took me by the hand to a police station, which was quite close by and asked me to repeat what I had told him to another policeman who was sitting behind a desk and who wrote something in a notebook, then led me through to a space behind the desk, a kind of office, I suppose, where there were two young women sitting at desks. I don't think they were policewomen. I suspect there was no such thing in 1937 – they were probably there in some kind of clerical or technical capacity. There was also a nice, fat tabby cat.

Being who they were and where they were, the young women probably had experience of lost children. One of them sensibly suggested I might want to go to the lavatory – a very good idea. Then they gave me a cup of milk and some biscuits, the desk sergeant found a piece of chocolate, and they asked if I liked cats. I assured them that I did, stroked their cat and told them about Joe.

They professed great interest and asked me if I could draw them a picture of him. They produced paper and coloured pencils (as I said, they obviously knew about children), and soon I was drawing pictures, writing little sentences and chatting away happily.

It seemed to me that Mum and Dad took their time coming to find me, though I knew they would come – they had said they would. I suspect that, when they first noticed I was missing, they all ran about like headless chickens for a while, though they always denied this. Anyway, Bob eventually led them to the police station. Doris, Wally, Peggy and Chum had gone straight home in case I was delivered there, and the rest of us followed, having thanked to police station staff for their care and kindness. I had a parent firmly clasping each hand right to the door of number 90.

Years later, recalling the episode, Mum told me that the desk sergeant had congratulated them on having such a sensible child. At the time, she told me I was a very silly girl to go wandering off like that. In my experience, British police are very good with small children and old ladies. If you happen to be an adult political demonstrator, it's a different story.

Apart from this one dramatic event, the week in Eastbourne passed quietly and pleasantly. The weather must have been good: in the photographs we have, we are all wearing summer clothes with never an umbrella or jumper in sight, and we spent quite a lot of time on the beach. A pebbly beach at high tide but, when the tide went out, a good stretch of sand was revealed for digging and building.

Wally and I enjoyed the sea, but Mum and Dad never ventured in. Neither of them had learned to swim, and I don't expect they had any suitable garments. Dad particularly enjoyed the company of his old friend, but the rest of us got along together pretty well too.

Back in Rothwell, it was unusual for me to have three weeks off school to spend with my friends and cousins. It had previously been straight home at the end of August and off to school. I quite enjoyed the change but I missed seeing Grandma and the rest of the family.

OUR BREAD was delivered six days a week by George, the Co-op roundsman, in his horse-drawn covered van. He carried the bread from van to door in a huge, square-shaped basket. We usually had a 'tin' loaf, baked in a loaf tin and therefore having a definite shape, easier and more economical to slice than the more free-form 'farm house' or 'bloomer' loaves.

My mother and both grandmothers were able, when occasion required it, to cut elegant, really thin bread and butter. This, of course, was ages before ready-sliced bread came onto the market. The secret is a loaf at least a day old, softened butter and a really sharp knife – and to cut horizontally rather than vertically. Our ordinary, everyday bread and butter was more thickly cut, both quicker and more economical. We paid for bread with bread checks – oval, copper-coloured pieces of metal that you bought at the Co-op with your groceries.

Milk was delivered daily, I think including Sundays, by Aunt Martha. Either she or her husband, Uncle Jim, was a cousin of either Grandpa or Grandma Andrew. They were tenant farmers of a farm about 20 minutes' away from our house. Aunt Martha and the milk came in an open, pony-drawn cart, the milk in large metal containers holding perhaps one and a half or two gallons, quite a weight when full.

Aunt Martha was a tiny woman, probably no more than five feet tall, attired winter and summer in a long, donkey-brown coat and a black, coal-scuttle hat. She wore a pair of no-nonsense glasses and a very serious expression. She would carry one of the milk cans to the doorstep and use a quarter-pint ladle to put the required amount into your milk jug.

Mum paid her in cash once a week. Both her pony and George's horse knew their rounds. They would automatically stop at the right gates, and needed only a flick of the rein to tell them to proceed when the driver was ready.

There was a lot of horse-drawn traffic still in the 1930s. Our rubbish was collected by horse and cart, and the rag and bone man used one. If one of the animals relieved itself in the street, someone would be out in a flash with a shovel and brush to collect the free fertiliser. Much of my adult life has been lived near Chelsea football ground and, when there is a match, a posse of mounted police is used for crowd control. It always grieves me to see the police horses' dung trodden heedlessly into the road. That wouldn't have happened in Littlewood Street seventy-odd years ago, that's for sure.

The only delivery ever made to our house by motorised vehicle was our annual supply of coal. This came in the Co-op coal lorry, driven by Mr Wells whose daughter was in my class at school. Mr Wells would unload our coal at the side of the road outside our back gate and, when Dad came home, he would transfer it in a wheelbarrow to the coal shed and stack it there.

The coal dust from the road and the garden path would be carefully swept up and reserved. It was an important component of the 'backing' bucket kept under the draining board in the kitchen. 'Backing' was a mixture of vegetable waste not suitable for the stock pot or rabbit food, damp tea-leaves, coal dust and anything else that could be used to damp down the fire and make the coal last longer. Most working class houses had a 'backing' bucket.

Sometimes an empty egg shell would be included by mistake in the 'backing' and, when it got hot, would explode, sending hot shards all over the place and making Peter and Joe dive for cover if they were about. The proper use for empty egg shells is to be placed, roughly crushed, at the base of plants to deter slugs and snails.

Our grocery order was delivered late on Friday afternoon by a boy on a bike with a very large basket in front. On Thursday evening,

Mum would write a list in her Co-op order book. As I have said, she was not particularly numerate, but she knew exactly what everything cost and exactly how much cash she had to lay out, and made sure that the two tallied. On Friday afternoon we took the book into the Co-op grocery shop. Mr Feakin, the manager, would make up the order and record the price of each item in the order book, total it all up and dispatch order and book with the boy.

Dad would check Mr Feakin's addition – it was always right – and on Saturday one of us would go to the shop, settle the bill, receive the divi slip and bring it safely home.

Newspapers – the *Daily Herald* on weekdays, *John Bull* weekly and *Reynolds News* on Sundays – were delivered early by a boy on a bike. The only other delivery I can recall was the post – two deliveries, one at breakfast time and a second at the end of the morning. Occasionally, if you posted something really early at Rothwell Post Office itself, it would be delivered by the second post the same day, but usually it came the next day.

The postal service was very important to us; it was for most people the only means of communication apart from personal contact. Very few people had telephones and, even for those who had, long distance (trunk) calls were tedious and time-consuming to make. The telegraph existed, of course, but telegrams were very expensive to send. I can remember our sending only one during my childhood (more of that later) and I don't think we ever received one.

So, when we arranged to see Uncle John's or Auntie Nell's family during our summer visit to the Forest, an exchange of letters –sometimes several – was necessary. Nevertheless, Mr Rowlatt, our postman, carried the post quite easily in a bag slung over his shoulder. There was no junk mail then; every letter counted, and there were not that many of them.

We certainly did not receive mail by every post. Mum and Grandma wrote to each other every week. Dad and Bob Horsman exchanged letters from time to time, and Dad got material relating to the Sons of Temperance. That was about it. Envelopes were carefully slit open to reveal the clean inside surface, and any page with a blank side was saved. These were used for drawing or for our pencil and paper games.

CHAPTER 8
Our food and how we ate

A LOT OF OUR FOOD was locally produced – as I have said, much of it as local as our own back garden or allotment. But food was imported too, mainly from the Empire, which still existed in the 1930s. Perversely, New Zealand lamb, 'Canterbury Lamb' as it was called, transported in refrigerated ships, was cheaper than locally produced and slaughtered lamb. We usually had half a leg of New Zealand lamb for dinner on Sunday, eked out with Yorkshire pudding and plenty of vegetables.

On Monday the lamb was eaten cold with pickles and boiled potatoes, usually preceded by a thin soup with the lamb bone as a basis. It made a final appearance as mince or shepherd's pie or rissoles or curry on Tuesday. Dinner on Wednesday, Thursday and Saturday varied according to what was available and cheap. If we had muscle meat, it was one of the very cheapest cuts: breast of lamb, say, stuffed and rolled and slow roasted, or stewed oxtail, or stewing beef made into a steamed steak and kidney pudding.

Rabbits were plentiful in season, and boys would often bring them round to sell at the door for sixpence each. You had to skin and paunch them, of course. You looked at your rabbit's ears. If the fur on them was still soft and downy, the rabbit would be tender enough to roast with sage and onion stuffing but, if the fur was bristly, you had best make your rabbit into a pie or stew it with suet dumplings. If you were lucky, the rag and bone man would come round in a day or two and give you a halfpenny for your rabbit skin.

Offal was cheap and was eaten much more often and in much greater variety than it is now. We often had stuffed, braised ox or sheep's heart for dinner, or liver – ox or pig's liver, not the more expensive and tender calf's or lamb's liver. Butchers in those days would prepare or semi-prepare various offal dishes, which you could finish or re-heat or eat as they were at home.

Faggots fairly often appeared at our mid-week dinners. The butcher would mince a mixture of pig's offal – liver, lights, spleen etc – and mix it with fat, breadcrumbs, onions and herbs and then wrap it in squares of pig's caul, a fatty membrane that enclosed the pig's intestines. The resulting parcels were then cooked and could be eaten cold or re-heated. Ours were served re-heated, so that the caul crisped up.

Then there was tripe, boiled for ages with onions. I hated it, both its appearance and its taste. And there were chitterlings – pig's intestines very thoroughly cleaned by the butcher or one of his underlings, soaked for a day or two in brine, then boiled for a long time. I hated them too, but we didn't have them for dinner. My parents ate them cold for tea.

Haslet was also a tea dish: a kind of offal meat loaf, wrapped in caul and baked. You could buy it either sliced or in a piece. As a child, I did not care for most offal dishes and often ate just vegetables and gravy. Many of the kinds of offal and cheaper cuts we ate in the 1930s are no longer available in butchers' shops or supermarkets or have to be specially ordered. I expect the bulk of that kind of thing goes into pet food now.

The butcher also made sausages, pork or beef, on site and also brawn. This was made from a pig's head, which would be boiled and then the meat from it mixed with some of the stock, which set to a firm jelly. This was also a tea dish.

On Fridays we had fish for dinner; everybody did, an ancient tradition that took a long time a-dying. The fish was either cod, which Mum fried in batter and served with home-made chips – my favourite dinner by a long chalk – or, if funds were low, herrings fried and served with boiled potatoes or kippers served with bread. If funds were healthy, one of these two last might be served for tea.

We always had a pudding at dinner-time, calorific and high carb, but we all used a lot of energy and did not get fat. On Sundays, when the oven was on, my mother made pastry, a big bowl of shortcrust. Some was used to make a fruit pie for Sunday dinner – apple, rhubarb, blackberry, raspberry, whatever was in season.

She often made a treacle tart too or a large jam tart and smaller jam tartlets – these were all for tea later in the week. She might also buy extra sausages and make sausage rolls, also for later teas.

As a young child, I was allowed to put the jam into the small tartlets and was given the pastry scraps to roll out with my miniature pastry board and rolling pin. After I had messed about with it for a bit , sometimes incorporating some jam or currants, my mother would bake it for me, and I would present it to my father to add to his mid-morning lunch. He never failed to tell me how much he had enjoyed it. (Mum also made him some rather more presentable fruit pasties to take.)

As I got older, I was shown how to cut out the pastry, then later how to roll it out and finally how to actually make it. By the time I was 12 or so, I could do the whole pastry operation by myself if need be and, when Mum was incapacitated before John was born, I did so quite confidently.

When the oven was on during the week, we often had a milk pudding: rice or tapioca, simply cooked in the oven in sweetened milk. An appetising brown crust would form on top and round the edges. Semolina pudding could be made on top of the stove and was usually served with a spoonful of home-made jam. Otherwise, we had steamed puddings: usually suet puddings.

In those days, suet didn't come shredded in a cardboard box. You bought it in a lump from the butcher. Mum would buy a sizeable lump and bury it in the flour bin. When making suet dough, she would cut off the amount of suet she needed, separate the small lumps from the connecting membrane (I liked to do this job as a small child). Then she chopped it with a sharp knife and a bit of flour to prevent its sticking to the knife.

The suet was then mixed with flour, water and a touch of baking powder to make a rather soft dough, which could either be rolled out to line and top a basin for fruit or steak and kidney puddings, or simply put into a basin in a lump on top of a few spoonfuls of Golden Syrup to make a treacle pudding, which was served with extra Golden Syrup at the table. Suet dumplings were made simply by putting balls of suet dough into a stew.

Our weekday breakfast was always the same. Mum would fry three slices of bread, three rashers of streaky bacon and two eggs. Mum and I shared an egg; the yolk was spread on my fried bread, and Mum had the white. Wally had a whole egg. Saturday breakfast was sometimes the same or sometimes boiled eggs with bread and butter. On Sundays we had beef sausages with fried tomatoes or sometimes mushrooms.

At tea-time, as well as the meaty or fishy dishes I have described, there would be home-grown salads in season: lettuce, radishes, tomatoes, spring onions and beetroot. The latter was boiled and served sliced and cold with malt vinegar – I didn't like it but most other people did. And there might be stewed fruit in season, with custard.

For Sunday tea, there would often be something out of a tin: salmon or sardines perhaps, or fruit of the more exotic variety, put into its tin, presumably, in South Africa or Australia – peaches or pineapple or apricots. We never saw any of this fruit fresh. Only fruit that could be picked unripe and allowed to ripen in the course of a sea voyage was imported fresh – oranges and bananas mainly.

In winter we might have something on toast for Sunday tea: perhaps scrambled eggs (known in Northamptonshire as 'buttered' eggs) or baked beans. We could only have toast when the fire was alight. Our gas stove had no grill, and we didn't have a toaster. I'm not sure if anybody had them. Most people had a toasting fork, and that was that.

In the week I often had tea at Auntie May's. Mum might meet me from school and take me there or I might go myself straight from school. Tea with my young cousins was nursery tea: bread and butter and things to spread on it – Marmite or honey or a very mild cheese spread or fish or meat paste – with sponge cake or biscuits perhaps to follow. Actually I preferred this to the more robust fare at home.

At bedtime, there would be a substantial snack: broth with bread, perhaps, or bread and dripping or breakfast cereal. Dad liked to have cheese for supper – we usually had Red Leicester, our local cheese.

As I have said, we shopped at the Co-op. There were three adjacent Co-op shops: the butcher's, run by Butcher Read, whose younger son John was in my class at school, then the grocer's, always referred to as 'The Stores', and then finally the baker's.

A lot of food was still sold loose. Bacon would be sliced to order on a hand-operated slicing machine. You chose your cut and thickness, and Mr Feakin or one of his assistants did the rest. Cheese was placed on a marble slab and sliced with a wire. Butter and lard were cut from large slabs. Biscuits were sold loose; you could buy packets but they were dearer. Broken biscuits were very cheap indeed. Flour, sugar and tea came ready packaged.

Eggs were simply put into a paper bag, so you had to be very careful with them. The specially formed papier mache egg containers we buy eggs in now did not appear until well after the war and seem to me to be one of very few sensible examples of modern packaging.

The manager of the baker's was a woman, Miss Wallington. You could buy bread here, of course, currant bread perhaps, and buns of various kinds and cakes and pastries. My female relatives were very scornful of shop-bought cakes and pastries and considered women who bought them to be lazy and inadequate housewives.

The only take-away fast food available to us was fish and chips. There were two fish and chip shops in Rothwell, both sold wet fish in the morning and cooked fish and chips from tea-time until well into the evening. Mr Munton's was the one nearest to us, but we could not afford to patronise him very often for family meals. Mostly, if a friend and I had a penny or even a halfpenny, we would buy a packet of chips ("with a few bits of batter, please" – and Mr Munton usually obliged if asked nicely).

Salt and malt vinegar were available on the counter to sprinkle on the chips, then we would poke a hole in the newspaper wrapping and eat the chips as we went along the street. Mr Munton cooked at dinner time too on Saturday but was, of course, closed on Sunday.

It was not only rabbit food that could be foraged for free. Food was available for human gatherers too. There were rights of way across many fields, and the hedges surrounding the fields were often covered with blackberry brambles. We usually made two or three serious blackberrying expeditions each year, taking suitable baskets or milk cans with us. The berries might be eaten raw or stewed with apple, or made into tarts or puddings or pies, or bottled or made into jam for winter consumption.

The same hedges often contained small crab-apple trees. The crab-apples were small and hard and sour. You couldn't eat them raw, but Mum made a delicious, clear, amber-coloured jelly from them, which we ate on bread or in tarts.

And there were mushrooms. We always looked out for them when we were out on walks, but Dad and I were the serious mushroomers. On a pleasant, warm Saturday evening, one of us would look at the other and say "How about mushrooming tomorrow?" and on the Sunday morning we would get up at about six, make a quick cup of tea and then set off on our bikes. We knew all the best places to go, and usually returned with enough mushrooms for a hearty breakfast and often some over for another meal. We continued this practice until I left home to go to university. We both enjoyed the still morning and the quiet companionship.

All of this free bounty was available in the late summer and early autumn, which was also the time for preparing jams and bottled fruit and pickles for the winter – pursuits still engaged in in the 1930s with almost medieval fervour. By the end of October the pantry was well stocked with enough preserves to see us through till the next summer.

Eggs were preserved too: they were cheaper and more plentiful in summer and could be preserved in water-glass (defined by the *New Shorter Oxford English Dictionary* as "an aqueous solution of sodium or potassium silicate ... used as a vehicle for fresco painting, as a fire-resistant paint, for pickling eggs etc"). This operation was undertaken by my father. I think the water-glass was dissolved in a bucketful of hot, possibly boiling, water, which was then allowed to cool. When it was quite cold, the eggs were totally immersed, a lid placed on the bucket and the bucket placed in the understairs storage space.

The eggs could be used for cakes and puddings and, at a pinch, for scrambling, but they were not suitable for boiling or frying or poaching.

CHAPTER 9
Housework and recycling

At 36 Littlewood Street we had one very modest, little rubbish bin, as had most of our friends and neighbours. Wealthier people tended to have bigger bins since it seemed they threw more stuff away. Our bin was often referred to as 'the ash bin' since, give or take an empty tin from Sunday tea, ash was often all it contained. Almost everything else was recycled. I have already told you about the stock-pot and the backing bucket, the pet rabbit and cat, the slug-repelling egg shells and the adult clothes unpicked and re-used to make children's clothes, but that is only the beginning of the story.

Sheets were turned sides to middle, ie they were cut from top to bottom down the worn middle section, the unworn sides were sewn together and became the new middle section. The worn ex-middle parts became the side tuck-in. When the sheets again became worn, the best parts could be made into tea-towels, handkerchiefs and pudding cloths. Any waste woollen cloth was cut into strips and used to make rag rugs. The strips were pulled through loosely woven sacking with a special peg. It was quite hard work, which both my parents took a hand to. The same technique was used to make rugs from odds and ends of knitting wool. These were softer and lighter than the rag rugs but not as hard wearing.

Worn out garments were used as dusters or polishing cloths. Finally, pieces of clean rag that we really could not put to any further use were put into the rag bag (Dad's old army kit bag), which was kept in the understairs store to await the rag and bone man. He came irregularly, seeking "any old rags, bottles, bones and rabbit skins".

We didn't have bottles. On the rare occasions we bought a bottle of any kind of soft drink, there would be a penny deposit on the bottle, returnable when it was taken back to the vendor. Of course, being a teetotal household, we had no beer bottles. If we had, I expect there would have been a penny deposit on each of them. In any case, I think that beer for home consumption was sold draught, decanted from a barrel into your own jug.

Our jam and pickling jars were washed and re-used year after year. Bones we had. Once they had been boiled clean in the stock-pot, they could be kept for a while. I expect the rag and bone man sold them on for making bone meal, and the rags for making 'shoddy', a kind of rough, felted cloth. Rabbit skins could only be kept for a day or two.

Newspapers had many future uses. My father would tear some of them into neat squares and hang them on a meat hook in the outside lavatory. He made fire-lighters by plaiting together neatly folded strips of newspaper, and he augmented our coal with 'snow balls' made by soaking newspapers in water, then pressing the pulp hard into balls, which were then allowed to dry out.

Mr Munton and the other fish shop used newspapers as outer wrappings for their wares and would give you a free bag of chips in exchange for a bundle, but we never had any to spare. I am not, of course, speaking of the multi-supplemented monster newspapers of today. In the 1930s papers were more manageable in size.

In the autumn, we would have two bonfires, one in the garden and one at the allotment, when the season's garden rubbish and detritus would be consumed. The ashes were dug back into the soil.

In the 1930s, of course, there were no plastic bottles and containers, no bubble wrap or other plastic packaging, no cooking foil or Tetra-pack or disposable nappies or the multitude of free newspapers, leaflets and advertising materials that today are collected by the council for re-cycling or that go to landfill.

In 2010, I can simultaneously wash our clothes and household linen, wash a day's pots and dishes and tidy up the living room carpet. Seventy years ago each of these was a formidable, time-consuming operation, for we had few electrical appliances. Washing, in particular, was a back-breaking, soul-destroying business.

Cotton whites had to be boiled first, and all cottons and linens were then subjected to the 'dolly tub' – put into a tub and pounded with the 'dolly stick' (a metal cone with holes in it, attached to a long stout stick) to agitate the washing to loosen the dirt. The washing then had to be rinsed in clean water, put through the mangle (two rollers, turned by hand, which squeezed out some of the water).

You could adjust the rollers, the closer they were together, the more water they squeezed out, but the harder the handle was to turn.

Some items – the collars and cuffs of 'good' white shirts and some tablecloths – were starched. The starch, Robin starch with a picture of a robin on the packet, came as a powder, which had to be first slaked with cold water, then 'turned' with boiling water, then thinned to the required consistency.

Then the washing had to be pegged out on the clothes line – everybody had a clothes line in their garden – and, if you were lucky, it more or less dried in the wind and fresh air. If it was raining, though, the washing had to be dried indoors. I think everyone who had a pre-war, working-class childhood remembers the sheer misery of a wet winter's washing day, steaming sheets all over the place, cold meat for dinner, mother cross and tired.

Washing day was Monday. Ironing was usually done on Tuesday. When I was a very young child, we still used flat irons, heavy metal irons that you heated on the fire or on the gas stove. When you thought the iron was hot enough, you spat on it and gauged the degree of readiness by the speed at which the saliva evaporated. Kettle-holders and iron-holders were a must at every fireside and gas stove side. The metal handles got very hot and could give you a nasty burn if handled carelessly. Little girls often knitted or sewed these holders as suitable Christmas or birthday presents for their female relatives. Pretty soon, though, we got an electric iron. I think it was our first electrical appliance.

Children were initiated into helping with the washing up at an early age. I think I was about five when I was taught to dry and put away the cutlery. Later came cups and saucers and tea plates, then the heavier stuff and finally the actual washing up.

Floors – mainly linoleum, but quarry tiles in the kitchen – had to be swept, washed and polished, and rugs taken outside and shaken. The rag rugs were very heavy to handle and held the dust and debris, needing a very vigorous shake. In those coal-fired days, dusting had to be done frequently and regularly, and again I was expected to help with this from an early age.

About Easter time, spring-cleaning took place. All the paintwork in the house was washed and polished, heavy furniture moved out so that the space behind it could be cleaned, pictures and mirrors were taken down and cleaned, and eventually we were fresh and clean and ready for the summer.

CHAPTER 10
Games and pastimes

THERE WERE quite a lot of group outdoor games, needing little or no equipment, played in the school playground before school or at playtime, or in the street in the evenings or at weekends, when there was hardly any traffic. Skipping could be a solitary exercise – most little girls had a skipping rope – but it was much more fun as a group activity.

Someone would produce a piece of rope several yards long, two girls would each take an end and twirl the rope between them. Other girls would run in and out of the field of activity, jumping over the rope and often singing skipping rhymes. Anyone who mistimed her jump and caused the twirling to stop had to take one end of the rope and let the erstwhile twirler join in the skipping.

There were several group singing games that involved a kind of tug of war. To play 'oranges and lemons', two girls would face each other, join hands and form an arch, having decided secretly which would be oranges and which lemons. The rest of the players would file singly through the arch, singing a version of the old Cockney rhyme:

> Oranges and lemons
> Say the bells of St Clement's
> I owe you five farthings
> Say the bells of St Martin's
> Here comes a candle to light you to bed
> Here comes a chopper to chop off your head
> Chop, chop, chop off the last man's head

At this point the arched arms would be quickly lowered and one of the players imprisoned within them. She would then, in a whispered consultation, have to choose between oranges and lemons and stand behind the appropriate person with her arms around her waist. This continued until all the players were lined up, when a tug of war would take place, and finally the two who had formed the arch would be pulled apart, and everyone would roll giggling on the ground. No one had to tell you how to play. You would have seen it played for as long as you could remember.

'Nuts in May' was another singing and tugging game. 'The farmer's in the dell' was also a singing game but no tugging was involved. We also played 'tic', known in other areas as 'chase' or 'he': a chasing game where the person who is 'it' or 'he' or 'on' tries to catch another player, who in turn becomes 'it'. These were all playground or party games as they required a fair number of players to be any fun.

In the street we skipped, of course, and played ball games or played 'Dicky', when two bricks were put a few inches apart and a short piece of wood placed across the gap. Armed with a longish stick, we would take turns to see who could flip the piece of wood, the 'Dicky', the farthest.

Skipping was a girls' game, but both sexes played 'Dicky', and both sexes played ball games, though boys tended to prefer cricket with 'stumps' chalked on a convenient wall and defended with a flat piece of wood, while girls usually preferred throwing a ball as high up as possible against a wall and performing some sort of action – clapping hands or spinning around on the spot, for instance – before catching the ball.

Boys played football too, the goal posts being indicated by a couple of coats or jumpers on the ground. Both sexes played 'Piggy in the middle' – two children would throw a ball to each other over the heads of several other children, who would jump up and try to intercept the ball.

We often went farther afield than our own street, for walks to fields where we knew there were trees to climb and brooks to paddle in or to the gates of Aunt Martha's and Uncle Jim's farmyard, where my

Groocock cousins and I took stale crusts to throw to make the hens come running, or to the recreation ground – 'the Rec" – to play on the swings and slides and see-saw and paddle in the hideously unhygienic paddling pool.

There wasn't a lot of space for indoor play at our house or Mary's or Josie's. There was more at Auntie May's. They had a kitchen big enough and warm enough to eat in as well as a separate dining-room, so there was a big, carpeted space in the drawing-room for floor play – building bricks or wheeled toys, for instance.

At Heather's house also there was more play space. They had a kind of back extension where her father grew potted plants, but there was a fair amount of floor space and table space too. We played role-playing games based on our everyday lives – mothers and fathers, shops, schools and also enactments of fairy tales.

We played board games – Snakes and Ladders, ludo, draughts and card games. Heather and I were keen on making things – dolls' clothes, kettle holders and such. We made a kind of paint by dissolving coloured sealing-wax in methylated spirits and decorated little pots and jars with it.

Heather's dad and his two brothers ran a small boot and shoe factory, and he would sometimes give us some scraps of softish leather, which we used to make little purses, comb cases, bookmarks and similar objects.

Once or twice, when we were ten or 11, we had our own little stall at the annual Dr Barnado's fund-raising bazaar. There was a rather timid little old lady – she was probably only in her 50s when we were children but we thought she was old – who lived in Rushton Road opposite to Auntie May. She was very fond of children – or at any rate of well behaved little girls. She was a bit wary of boys and was absolutely terrified of dogs. She ran the Dr Barnado's charity in Rothwell and was delighted to have our help and our company. I think she was probably quite lonely.

When I was a very little child, I liked to be read to, and my mother liked to read aloud. The trouble was I liked to have the same few stories over and over again, while she would have preferred a change once in a while. Still, she bore with me. I liked to sit on her lap, holding a cuddly toy and looking at the book she was reading from. If she deviated from the text, I always knew and complained.

Talking of cuddly toys, mine were rabbits. I had dolls and loved them and tended them carefully, but they were made of hard materials and were cold to touch. My rabbits were soft and warm – just the thing to hold when you were listening to a story or falling asleep. There were three of them. The oldest and smallest was Little Bunny Mauve, a small rabbit couchant with a coat of soft mauve plush. Then there was Bad Bunny Bags. I think he must have been named for a story book character. He was a rabbit rampant, or at least sitting up on his bottom with all four paws stretched out in front of him. He had a white front and red back, head and ears. And a white tail, of course.

Finally there was Common Brown Trout, again a rabbit couchant, cream in colour with a big, light brown patch on each side. At the time he joined my menagerie, Wally was collecting a set of freshwater fish cigarette cards, and I thought my rabbit looked very like a common brown trout.

Once, when I was little, someone gave me some money to buy a doll – it might have been a 4th birthday present. Dad and I went off to Kettering to buy a doll at Curry's, which in those days sold toys and all manner of other things. Mum didn't come, I think probably because Wally was ill. Anyway, I fell in love, not with a doll but with a bright green, quite large, rubber frog. Although he was made of rubber, his skin was soft and textured and quite warm to touch, and I wanted him with all my heart. So we bought him. Mum was surprised, and I think a bit put out, but she accepted him into the household. I called him Toad, and he joined my rabbits for story reading and bedtime.

We played quite a lot of pencil and paper games, and every bit of paper that could be written or drawn on was carefully saved. We had a smallish, lined writing pad, but that was only used for writing proper letters. I don't remember that we ever bought any other paper. There were the perennial children's games: Noughts and Crosses, Boxes, Hangman and one or two others played less commonly and over a wider age range. If a game of Baker's Dozen, for instance, was proposed, teenagers and grown-ups might well join in.

The players would between them compile a list of 13 categories – town, country, famous man, famous woman, colour, animal etc – then someone would randomly select a letter, closing their eyes and bringing a pencil down on the page of a book or newspaper. Then the players had to write down one of each category beginning with that letter. The game ended when one of the players completed their 13 – or when everyone agreed that they couldn't do any more. Then the players would in turn call out what they had written down. If you had thought of the same answer as someone else, you both had to cross that one out. The winner was the player with the most original answers.

A variation of this game was to select a category, animals, say, and to write down one beginning with each letter of the alphabet: anteater, buffalo, cow etc.

Cigarette cards, also known as fag cards or 'photes', were an important part of our childhood. Most men, but hardly any women, smoked in those days, though among the working class few could afford to smoke heavily. When he was on the dole or short time, my dad would sometimes smoke just one a day. He would smoke half of it, carefully stub it out and save the rest for later. Dad and Grandpa and Len all smoked Woodbines, they were the cheapest of the more well known brands. They came in rather lurid, orange and green packaging – fives in a paper packet, tens and 20s in cardboard packets. Only the tens and 20s contained cigarette cards.

The cards were issued in themed sets of 50 – wild flowers, say, or wild animals, or kings and queens – and a set would run for a limited period, but I don't remember how long it was. Each card had a picture on one side and information about it on the other. In each set, some cards were much rarer than others, and a lot of swapping and trading went on. Some bolder children would hang about outside newsagents, where most cigarettes were sold and, when a man emerged with a packet of cigarettes, would ask "Can I have the phote, please, Mister?". It would usually be handed over unless the Mister had someone at home with a better claim.

You could buy for a few pence albums, produced by the cigarette manufacturers, in which to mount your collection – a new album for each set – with a place for each card and the information from the back of the card printed underneath. Enterprising groups of three or four children would sometimes organise a 'Phote-a-Go' – a mini fair on the pavement with games involving rolling marbles or flicking cards or other simple challenges. You paid a phote to have a turn at one of the games and, if you were successful, your prize was several photes. News would go round the school like wild fire one afternoon: "Photo-a-Go in Fox Street after tea", and a good crowd would turn up with their spare photes.

Wally was a keen collector of cigarette cards until he was 12 or so. He went to a lot of trouble to secure full sets and stick them carefully into the appropriate albums. I don't know what happened to them eventually. I was never an avid collector, nor were Mary, Heather or Josie, though we liked to have a few spare photes for the 'Phote-a-Goes'. My Groocock cousins were too young to be interested in collecting.

'Phote' must have been a diminutive of 'photograph', though I didn't realise that at the time. Cigarette cards disappeared with the war and never made a come-back but they were a cunning ploy. Children encouraged their men folk to smoke and to stick to the same brand.

Wally and most of his friends were keen train spotters. There was no railway station in Rothwell but there were stations in Kettering and Desborough and Rushton, a village about a mile and a half from Rothwell, so there were quite a lot of railway tracks within easy reach. By the 1930s there were four railway companies in Great Britain: the London Midland and Scottish (LMS), the London North Eastern (LNER), the Great Western (GWR) and the Southern (SR).

Each company produced its own rolling stock, and each locomotive (all steam-powered then) had a number, and some had names. All the neighbouring stations were on the LMS lines, so the boys mostly collected data about LMS engines, but sometimes on a bank holiday we would make a family expedition to a place called Roade, where there was a picnic spot near the LNER lines, so Wally got some kind of kudos from having LNER engines in his collection.

When we went to the Forest, we travelled GWR from Birmingham, and the year we went to Eastbourne we travelled SR. Dad got quite interested and kept his own record, but Mum and I never summonsed up any enthusiasm. We liked the trips and the picnics, though, and might look for wild flowers or make daisy chains or play 'I spy'.

There was one cinema in Rothwell and several in Kettering, but we were not great cinema-goers. It was very much a special occasion thing. The Odeon cinema in Kettering put on special, cheap Saturday morning showings for children, who had a special song to sing. We never went. The admission charge plus the bus fare to Kettering put it beyond our means, but we knew the words:

> Every Saturday morning, where do we go?
> Getting into mischief? Oh dear, no!
> Join the Mickey Mouse Club, This will be our song.
> Every Saturday morning at the O-DE-ON !

We had a rival version that went:

Every Saturday morning, where do we go?
Stuffing off to pictures? Oh dear, no!

CHAPTER 11
Special occasions

CHRISTMAS preparations began about a month or more ahead. The last Sunday in November was traditionally 'stir up Sunday' but we often began before. We started with the puddings, which required quite a bit of preparatory work before the actual mixing. Raisins usually had to be de-pipped, currants needed to be cleaned and picked over for stalks and foreign bodies, almonds had to be blanched, suet chopped, candied peel prepared and bread crumbs grated. Then you could put it all together with the flour, brown sugar and spices and mix in the eggs and milk.

Everyone had to have a stir and make a secret wish. Joe and Peter were in turn lifted up, indignant and complaining, and helped to stir – wishing, no doubt, that these daft humans would stop their silly games and let a decent, self-respecting cat and rabbit get on with their lives in peace. For goodness' sake, they didn't even like Christmas pudding.

Actually, neither did I, but I always took a very small portion, because Christmas pudding came with threepenny bits: tiny, silver coins, affectionately known as 'Joeys', smaller even than the present five-penny pieces but a lot more use than five pence today. With a threepenny bit, you could buy six half-penny portions of chips from Mr Munton, or a child's return bus ticket to Kettering, or a horribly dangerous, flammable celluloid toy, or a packet of five sparklers – well worth eating a little bit of Christmas pudding for.

Strangely, my miniscule portion always contained a threepenny bit. So did Wally's, but he liked Christmas pudding and always accepted a man-sized piece.

But back to the mixing bowl. The pudding mixture was covered with a clean cloth and left to mature overnight. Then next morning it was given a final stir, decanted into basins, covered with greaseproof paper and pudding cloths, and steamed for seven or eight hours. When cooled, the puddings were covered with clean pudding cloths and stored until needed, when a further three hours' steaming was required. No wonder there's a brisk market nowadays for ready-made puddings!

Making the cake came next, though not usually on the same day. Fruit and nuts needed to be prepared in the same way, and the mixture was baked in a slow oven heat for three hours or so. When quite cold, it was put in a tin and stored, ready for icing a few days before Christmas.

My mother was a very skilled cake decorator, a talent which my daughter Harriet seems to have inherited. My own efforts are very rough and ready in comparison. Mum had a full set of icing equipment, including a turntable, and was able to produce the most elaborate scroll work and rosettes and writing, She did Auntie May's Christmas cake too, and decorated birthday cakes for all the cousins as well as for us.

Then there was the mincemeat – dried fruit, grated apple, suet, sugar and spices, mixed and put into jars to mature for a few weeks. In our family, we traditionally made the first mince pies on Christmas Eve. As a little child, I was allowed to spoon the mincemeat into pastry cases, then, when Mum had put the lids on and glazed them with egg, I would sprinkle a little sugar on top before they went into the oven. By the time I was a teenager, I played an equal part in the operation.

We would put on the wireless and listen to the festival of lessons and carols from King's College, Cambridge, as we worked, and sometimes Dad found a job he could do indoors so that he could listen with us. Sometimes Mum and I sang along with the carols, but that was not a very good idea. Neither of us could sing in tune, and King's College choir did much better without us. We made good mince pies, though.

When we were little, Grandma and Grandpa came round on Christmas Eve evening to see us hang up our stockings by the fireplace. I think they enjoyed seeing us all excited and eager for once to go to bed, but unable to get to sleep for ages. Our filled stockings and presents were placed beside our beds when we had at last gone to sleep and were opened first thing on Christmas morning in our parents' bedroom.

Grandma and Grandpa came round again in the morning, Grandma to help with the dinner and Grandpa to help play with any new toys. We would have a fire in the front room, and both the front room and the living-room were decorated with coloured paper garlands and streamers. We had a very small Christmas tree, which stood on the sewing-machine – there was no space for a floor-standing one.

Christmas dinner was a big event. Usually, we had a large chicken but sometimes a joint of pork, eked out in either case with Yorkshire pudding and stuffing and supported by roast potatoes, brussels and carrots. Then, of course, there was the pudding with threepenny bits and custard. And then mince pies with tea and crackers.

Joe would be given some of the meat with vegetables and gravy, and Peter had two or three whole, raw Brussels sprouts, not just the outer leaves, which were his usual portion. Since they didn't like pudding, Peter had some grape nuts and Joe a saucer of milk. Truth to tell, Joe probably preferred his meat raw and newly killed, and Peter was not bothered which part of the brussels he ate, but we liked to have them join us, and they tolerated our quaint habits, though they drew the line at being helped to pull crackers or wear paper hats.

After dinner and washing up, we played games – card games or pencil and paper games and a game called 'Tell me', a kind of embryonic Trivial Pursuits – and, of course, we all wore paper hats from the crackers. Sometimes we listened to something on the wireless, but not to the King's broadcast – we were not royalists. Somehow we managed to eat a huge tea and went to bed feeling very full indeed.

On Boxing Day it happened all over again! In the morning, Mum, Wally and I went round to Auntie May's, and Dad went off to join his fellow Mission bandsmen to play carols around the town. He joined us later at dinner-time. There was always turkey for dinner at Auntie May's on Boxing Day, and the cousins would have new toys to play with. We would take one or two of our presents round there too.

On 27 December normal life resumed. Dad went back to work if there was work to go to, and the domestic routine was picked up again, though school holidays continued for a few days more. We didn't do New Year. There were no fireworks or parties to mark it. People sometimes wished each other a Happy New Year, but that was all.

My birthday on 2 March was always marked by a party for my friends and cousins. There would be a birthday tea with cake and candles, followed by party games. Each guest brought a little present, but there were no party bags to be taken home at the end. They are a fairly recent innovation. In fact, birthday parties happened quite frequently – most children would have one – and they followed more or less the same pattern.

Shrove Tuesday, Pancake Day, was sometimes before and sometimes after my birthday, depending on when Easter fell. We always had pancakes and ate them at tea-time, when there was more time to cook and savour them. Mum made a big jug of batter, and we ate the pancakes in turn as soon as they came out of the pan and were rolled up with a sprinkle of sugar and a squeeze of lemon.

Palm Sunday, the Sunday before Easter, was Fig and Prune Sunday, when everyone had stewed, dried figs and prunes with cold custard for tea. It doesn't sound very nice, but actually was quite pleasant. I thought so, anyway. I have never been able to find out the origin of this custom, which has long since died out.

On one of the days between Palm Sunday and Good Friday, in

some years the chapel choir would put on a performance of one of the Easter oratorios, Stainer's Crucifixion or Olivet to Calgary. They rehearsed for weeks and imported a professional soloist for the occasion. It would be an evening performance, and the chapel was packed. We always went. It was a real occasion. You wore your Sunday clothes and saw most of your extended family and friends there. I don't think there was an admission charge but there was probably a collection.

Then there was Good Friday – hot cross buns from the Co-op bakery for tea – and Easter Sunday, with boiled eggs for breakfast with our names written on them and lots of chocolate eggs, often presented in an egg cup or teacup or mug. It was the usual custom for aunts, uncles, grandparents and parents to give Easter eggs to children, and I used to feel rather daunted by all that chocolate. I have never, even as a child, had a 'sweet tooth', but fortunately my dad liked chocolate and helped me out.

Whitsun rather passed us by in Rothwell, where we had a special arrangement. Trinity Sunday, the Sunday after Whitsun, was Ro'well Fair Sunday (Ro'well, pronounced as in bread roll, is an ancient contraction of Rothwell, still almost universally used by its inhabitants). Way back, in 1204, King John granted Ro'well a charter, entitling the town to hold an annual fair 'at the Feast of Holy Trinity for and during five days'. 'Granted' is probably a euphemism. I suspect that John, that impecunious monarch, extracted payment for the charter.

Originally the purpose of the fair was the buying and selling of farm stock and later the hiring of labour, but this had died out by the 1930s, and it had become purely a fun-fair. It was stipulated that the fair should be proclaimed by the Lord of the Manor's bailiff on the Monday following Trinity Sunday.

On Ro'well Fair Monday morning, the first proclamation is read outside the manor house as soon as the nearby church clock has finished striking six. Three ragged cheers follow the "God save the King and the Lord of the Manor" with which the charter concludes, and the attendant band then plays the national anthem. The bailiff is mounted on a horse and attended by a number of halberdiers carrying halberds denoting the reigns of some, but not all, monarchs since the time of King John.

The fair is proclaimed outside each of the eight or so pubs in the town, and the bailiff is regaled at each with a rum toddy. Young men vie with each other to try to capture the halberds, and quite often things got quite rough and out of hand in the days when my friends and I attended as children and teenagers.

In 2005 for the first time in half a century or so, I went to see the fair proclaimed again. Chris and I went to Kettering to stay with John and Jenny for the weekend, and we all got up in time to get to Rothwell Manor House by 6 o'clock. John and I agreed that it was quite a tame affair compared to the ones we remembered.

So, while workplaces all over the country closed for the Whit Monday bank holiday and schools generally had a week's holiday, we in Rothwell soldiered on. Ro'well Fair week was our celebration: the factories closed on the Monday, and the schools for the whole week. On the preceding Thursday and Friday wagons would arrive loaded with all the paraphernalia needed to set up the rides, stalls and side-shows. There were huge, mobile steam engines which generated power for the rides, and caravans in which the fair families travelled and lived. The centre of the town was a hive of activity as the fair was set up – it was almost as exciting as having the fair fully operational.

On the Saturday before Trinity Sunday most of the attractions opened up in the evening and did a good trade for most people went down to have a look around. On Trinity Sunday afternoon the vicar officiated at an open-air service, blessing the fair from the steps of one of the roundabouts. Afterwards we went home for a tea that included Ro'well Fair tarts, raspberry jam tarts with a topping of milk curd, ground almonds and egg.

On the Monday the fair was open all day, but my parents did not come down until the afternoon. Monday was wash day, Ro'well Fair or no Ro'well Fair. The fair week was the only time we saw coconuts – there was a coconut shy but no one in my family was any good at ball games. You could, however, buy a coconut and carry it nonchalantly in your hand up the road. There were also Ro'well Fair rock and brandy snaps on sale – all exotic, once-a-year fare. Peashooters, often homemade from a hollowed-out piece of elder wood, were much in evidence during Ro'well Fair week.

We children were sad to see the fair pack up and move on at the end of the week, but I think our parents were quite relieved. The constant badgering for pennies for this and that would have been a bit wearing in those straitened times.

The August Bank Holiday (the first Monday in August in those days) saw us in our beloved Forest of Dean, usually taking part in a big family picnic, but there was no special ritual involved.

We didn't do Halloe'en. I think that was a post-war import from the United States. Guy Fawkes night was a much more low-key affair than it is now. My cousins and I rather fearfully held lighted sparklers in a darkened room after tea, and Uncle Irvie would set off a few modest fireworks at a safe distance from the house.

Armistice Day was solemnly marked until the beginning of the second world war. At school, Mr Briers, our headmaster, not a great man for marking solemn occasions, would nevertheless say a few words about this one at morning assembly. A minute before 11 o'clock our class teacher would have us all standing beside our desks and, as we heard the church clock begin to chime, we bowed our heads, shut our eyes and stood absolutely still and quiet for two long minutes. Our teacher told us when we could relax again.

And that brings us round to Christmas again!

*Grandpa Kirby in his footman's uniform at Launde
Abbey. Probably 1888 or 1889*

Wally and me. Summer 1930

*Dad's family about 1920.
Grandma, Len, Dad, Charlie, Grandpa*

*Uncle Tom and me.
Summer 1932*

Silly games with Uncle Jack Elliot's motor bike. Mum and Wally on the bike; Dad and me in the side-car. Albert Road, Coleford, summer 1932

Wood gathering with Grandma Kirby. Probably summer 1933

Severn Bridge. Wally, Grandma Kirby, Dad. 1935 or 1936

Dad at ease in the Forest of Dean. 1935 or 1936

Auntie Rene, Wally and me picking raspberries in the Forest. Summer 1932 or 1933

Nelia's sixth birthday party. From left: Nelia's cousin from Kettering, Christine, June, Nelia, Audrey, and me

Postcard from Nelia with photograph of her birthday party. The postage was only one penny

*Mum in her St John Ambulance uniform.
Probably 1942 or 1944*

*Mum and Larry with birthday cake. He
supplied the ingredients, she the baking
skills. I don't remember whose birthday it
was. Summer 1944*

Baby brother John. Late 1944

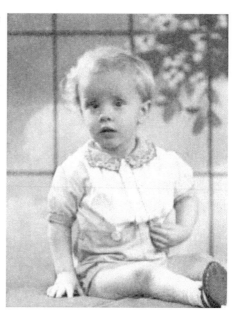

At Rothwell rec, probably summer 1944. From left to right: Auntie Rene, Wally, Elizabeth, Ann, Mum, me

Upper and Lower Sixth with Miss Woodrow. Summer 1947. I am on Miss Woodrow's left

Higher School Certificate Latin group with Mr Cooke. From left: Gladys, Fay, me, Mavis. 1947 or 1948

I STARTED SCHOOL in September 1934, aged four and a half. I knew about school. Wally, Mary, Josie and Heather Taylor, being older than me, all went, as did a number of neighbouring children, and on the whole they gave it a good press. I was quite prepared to give it a go and set out confidently with my mother on the first morning. 'School' for me that morning was Rothwell Victoria Infants School, a single-storey, red-brick, late 19th century School Board building, comprising three class-rooms round an assembly hall and cloakroom facilities.

There was quite a large playground, containing at some distance from the school building two sets of lavatories, one for girls and one for boys. If you needed the lavatory during lesson time, the rather coy formula was "Please may I go across the yard?" I don't remember its ever being queried or refused.

Schools and teachers were, of course, in many ways very different in 1934 from those of today, but there are one or two particular things I want to mention. In the 19th and early 20th centuries there had been something called 'the pupil teacher system' whereby a promising 13-year-old, whose parents were prepared to let her or him stay at school beyond the statutory leaving age, could serve a kind of apprenticeship.

If the course was satisfactorily completed, they could become certificated teachers. The system was discontinued after the first world war, but in 1934 there were still a number of teachers who had come up by this route working in schools alongside college-trained colleagues, and very good teachers they were too.

Second, women teachers had to retire upon getting married, though, if later widowed, they might return. This silly rule had to be abandoned during the second world war, when many male teachers were conscripted into the armed forces.

Third, women teachers were paid less than men with the same experience and responsibilities. I think the fraction was five sixths. This continued after the war and was still in operation when I started teaching in the 1950s. The National Union of Teachers had been fighting for equal pay since 1919. It was agreed in 1955 and phased in over the next five to six years.

But back to September 1934. My mother completed the formalities, told me that I was to come home at dinner time with Mary and Josie, kissed me good bye and left me in a class-room with between 30 and 40 other rising fives. The teacher in charge of the reception class (known colloquially as the 'babies class') was Mrs Barrs. Yes, Mrs! She was a widowed lady who was also a mother – she had a grown-up daughter called Gwen.

Little children, in their inexperience, accept as the norm whatever comes their way. It was only much later that I realised what lucky children we were to be introduced to the world of school by motherly, experienced Mrs Barrs. I have heard stories of contemporaries who preferred to wet their pants rather than ask permission to go to the lavatory. Kind Mrs Barrs would often approach a wriggling child and murmur discreetly "Do you want to go across the yard, dear?"

The class in which I found myself was unusual in that there was a considerable gender imbalance, only ten girls and well over 20, nearly 30 boys, five of them called John, which must have been the name of the year in 1930. In most classes the sexes were more evenly balanced. I remember all ten girls: Margaret, Marjorie, Sonia, Audrey, June, Nita, Christine, Barbara, Nelia and me.

As I have said, the Co-op butcher's son and the Co-op coalman's daughter were in my class. One girl was a farmer's daughter, one boy a farm worker's son, one girl's father was a printer and two children had fathers running businesses connected with the boot and shoe trade. Everybody else's parent worked, when they could, in boot and shoe factories.

Our induction to school with Mrs Barrs was quite gentle. We had little, individual blackboards with rubbers and coloured chalks. We had individual sand trays to make houses and gardens and quite a lot of mess, I think. During that year we learned the relationship of, say, the spoken word 'four', the written symbol '4' and the physical reality of four counters. Mrs Barrs read to us, and we played singing games. Thursday afternoon was 'book day', and Friday afternoon 'toy day', when we could bring something from home. Mornings started with a whole school assembly, as was the law, conducted by Miss Green, the headmistress.

I don't remember any other religious content to our education at the infants' school. If there was anything else, it has left no impression on me.

Parents who wanted to could buy 'morning milk' for their children. Little bottles of milk, each containing one third of a pint, were delivered in crates to the school and distributed at the beginning of morning playtime. A bottle of milk cost a ha'penny. My parents insisted that I should have it, so I took two pence ha'penny to give to my teacher each Monday morning. There was a perforation in the cardboard cover to the bottle through which you inserted a straw. When you had drunk some of the milk, you could blow bubbles in what was left, but most teachers discouraged this.

I continued to drink 'morning milk' throughout my school life. When Ellen Wilkinson's 1946 School Milk Act was passed, milk was provided free for all schoolchildren under 18, but this concession was abolished when Margaret Thatcher became Education Secretary in the Heath government. Her Education (Milk) Act 1971 abolished free milk for children over seven, earning her the chant "Maggie Thatcher Milk Snatcher" at political rallies. I have heard it said that she found this sobriquet hurtful. I hope that is true.

From Mrs Barrs, we passed into the hands of Miss Harris, who, I think, came up by the pupil-teacher route. She was a middle-aged woman who shared a rather nice house in the middle of the town with her sister, Miss Rowena. In Miss Harris' class-room there was a strip of blackboard, about a yard deep, all around the walls at the right height for children of our age to stand at and draw. We still had our little, individual, portable blackboards and rubbers for work, and Miss Harris had a free-standing blackboard and easel at the front of the room.

Not surprisingly, the room was almost always filled with a floating cloud of chalk dust. I am surprised that Miss Harris didn't suffer from some kind of industrial complaint from breathing in the dust year after year, but she always seemed pretty well. Miss Harris was quicker, sharper and crisper than Mrs Barrs and inclined to smack if someone made her cross. Corporal punishment was taken for granted in schools at that time but, in my experience, was not handed out excessively. Certainly I and many of my contemporaries survived our education without chastisement.

It fell to Miss Harris to introduce us to the skill of reading. Some of the class, including me, had more or less got the hang of it already from being read to at home. To others it was completely virgin territory. We were taught by the phonetic method, and Miss Harris told us a little story around each letter, incorporating the sound of the letter. It was class teaching, chalk and talk, and it worked better for some than for others.

I don't really remember our number work with Miss Harris but there must have been some for most of us could manage 'adding up' and 'taking away' without counters by the end of the year.

The top infants' class was taken by Miss Green, the headmistress, who was college trained. We were all rather in awe of Miss Green, who was quite strict and inclined to come down hard on any playfulness or whispering in class.

We now progressed to pencil and paper in little exercise books, lined for writing and squared for sums. We began to write short sentences, and Miss Green would hear us read individually.

We were now ready, aged seven, to move on to Gladstone Street Council School – 'the Big School' as it was usually called. This was another end-of-the-19th-century school board building, and the board must have been very parsimonious or very hard up or both. It is, I think, the only school building I have ever been into (and I have been into quite a few) that had no separate assembly hall, and there was the absolute minimum of circulation space.

Essentially, the building consisted of a long corridor with rooms on each side. Along one side, there were five class-rooms, cheek by jowl, and between two of them there was a folding partition, which was opened each morning to create a space big enough for the whole school to squeeze into for the obligatory assembly. Afterwards, the partition was closed, and the rooms reverted to being teaching spaces.

On the other side of the corridor was a boys' cloakroom with entrance from the boys' playground, a class-room, a poky little head's office, a girls' cloakroom with entrance from the girls' playground and another class-room. You will note that the playgrounds were now gender-separated – the Victorians took no chances with their 7-14-year-olds. There was a set of lavatories in each playground, and here the accepted formula for using them during lesson time was "Please may I leave the room?" Again, I don't remember that the request was ever refused.

Alongside the school was an extensive garden where senior boys were taught gardening skills, and part of the garden was occupied by a single-storey addition to the school known as the Cookery Room, built, I think, in response to the 1926 Hadow report on *The Education of Adolescents*. Although it was called the Cookery Room, it was, in fact, fitted out with equipment for the practical teaching of both domestic science and woodwork by peripatetic teachers to senior girls and boys respectively.

The room had a third, occasional use as a dental surgery when the school dentist visited. Parents could choose to use this service, which was free, and my parents chose to use it. The dentist made one visit to examine and recommend treatment, and came again later to carry out the treatment. I had one or two small fillings, without injections, at the hands of the school dentist, but my baby teeth were pretty good – as I have already said, I didn't have a 'sweet tooth'.

There was no staff room. Teachers gathered in one of the classrooms at playtimes and, if they were not Rothwell residents, at dinner time as well.

The sole aim of 'the Big School' – for the first four years anyway – was success in the scholarship examination, taken, as I have said, in March of the school year in which your 11th birthday fell. Good results in this examination seems to have been the main – possibly the only – criterion by which council schools were judged. Mr Briers had seven fulltime teachers, including himself, to deploy and used five of them to cover the first four years.

When we first went up to the Gladstone Street school, our class was still a unit, known as 'standard one'. The 19th century nomenclature still endured. Miss Tye had been in charge of standard one for many years. She had been a young pupil-teacher when Dad, Charlie – and Len were schoolboys so, by the time I arrived in her classroom, she was middle aged and knew her pupils inside out. She knew where we fitted into our community, what our families were like, when to be very firm and when to turn an occasional blind eye. She was one of the best teachers I have known in a lifetime spent in education.

We had many new skills to learn. For a start we had to learn to do 'real writing', which is what we called cursive script. In the infants school we had printed our letters. The front wall of Miss Tye's classroom was almost covered by a large, fixed blackboard, across the top of which was written the alphabet in capital letters and in a line beneath in lower-case letters. We had to practise writing these, and we had to get used to using a pen and ink. The pen-holder was a short orange coloured stick with a metal band around it at one end, and a pen nib was inserted between the metal and the wood. The pen-holder was pretty well indestructible but the nibs often got broken or 'crossed' and had to be replaced.

All the teachers had a box of pen nibs in their desks. The ink was contained in little, pottery ink wells that fitted into holes in our desks.

The ink wells were replenished every Monday morning by big boys from the top class. These big boys seemed to do a lot of jobs about the place that nowadays would be done by a school-keeper. For instance, they opened and closed the partition that made two classrooms into an assembly space.

Some children made very heavy weather of the pen and ink business, and inky hands were commonplace. We all had little squares of blotting paper to limit the damage. My dad had a bottle of black ink and one of red in his bureau at home for doing his Sons of Temperance records and had sometimes let me experiment, carefully supervised, with pen and ink, so I knew it could be a tricky business, but both my dad and Miss Tye were very patient.

Down the left-hand side of the board was written the multiplication table that we were learning at the moment. We learned the tables by rote, chanting them in unison, and by the end of our year in standard one we could do the lot from 'one two is two' to the triumphant end 'twelve twelves are a hundred and forty four'. Some children were quite probably carried along in the chorus, but the system certainly worked for me. Even today, if someone says to me 'Seven eights?' or 'Nine sixes?' or whatever, I can usually answer at once without even thinking about it.

In the big school the girls were taught needlework, or 'sewing' as we called it, by Miss Tye. The girls from standards one and two were combined, and the boys did 'handwork', presumably with the standard two teacher. We girls started off by making pretty little things: table centres and runners, antimacassars and the like. Miss Tye taught us simple embroidery stitches, and we could buy the finished articles at cost price. They were usually destined to be presents for aunties and grandmas. The boys made things like blotters and bookmarks, which also ended up as presents. The sewing/handwork business happened on at least two, possibly three, afternoons a week in the time before afternoon playtime. We eventually progressed to making plainer, more useful items. I remember making a little dirndl skirt when I was nine or ten.

Sewing time was a very pleasant time. Miss Tye was patient and relaxed and did not expect us to stitch away in grim silence: quiet chatting was permitted as long as we got on with our work. It was the custom, and had been for years, to take sweets to sewing lessons, if you could afford to, and hand them round discreetly to your friends. We thought Miss Tye didn't know, but I'm sure Miss Tye knew perfectly well what was going on and chose to turn a blind eye. I have done the same thing myself. I don't see much harm in a wine gum or small boiled sweet lodged quietly between cheek and gum. Aggressive gum chewing is another thing altogether and not to be tolerated.

My dad was well aware of the sweet sucking culture and would sometimes quietly slip me a halfpenny at dinner time on sewing days. Despite not being that keen on sweets, I would buy and bring along my contribution. I don't know if my mother knew about the halfpennies, but I fancy she didn't. Unlike Miss Tye, Mum was not renowned for turning a blind eye. That is one of the many things I wish I had asked her while there was still time.

Another innovation at the big school was swimming, an optional extra and not a very popular one. Swimming lessons took place at the Rothwell local authority swimming-pool, down at the bottom of the recreation ground, a good mile's downhill walk, I should think, from school and a long uphill walk home afterwards. The pool was an open-air one and, although swimming lessons were confined to the summer term, the air and the water were usually pretty cold. I'm sure the water was adequately filtered and perfectly safe but it looked uninviting. The modern practice of painting the insides of swimming-pools a pretty blue had not yet arrived, and our swimming water looked greenish, brown and murky.

At the beginning of the summer term, we were given notes to take home explaining the swimming option and inviting our parents to take it up. Mary, Josie and Heather had all, when it was their turn to take the notes home, managed to persuade their parents against swimming lessons and strongly advised me to do the same. What a hope! "Of course you are going" my mother said bracingly. "You are a very lucky girl to have the chance. Don't be so chicken-hearted!". This was an epithet she applied to anybody she thought was being a bit of a wimp. I don't think I have heard anyone else use it, but she must have picked it up from somewhere. Anyway, of course, I went to swimming lessons, and it was not a joyful experience.

Only two other girls from my class, Audrey and Nita, took up the option. The three of us and the rest of the pupils from the whole school who had opted for swimming lessons but were not yet able to swim were put together in one group.

The swimming instructor, Mrs Cross, was a formidable lady, a powerful swimmer and also a vocal soloist, in which capacity she was known as 'Madam Parkes', her maiden name. She had a good, loud voice for issuing swimming instructions. She had us all lying on our tummies on the cold concrete surround to the pool while she took us through the arm and leg movements required for the breast stroke, her preferred stroke. She thought the front crawl 'inelegant'.

So there we were: arms first, forward, turn, out, in. When she was satisfied with our arm movements, we progressed to legs: wide, close, bend. Then we had to remember both movements and put them together. After that we got into the water and tried it out for real. As soon as anyone could manage a few strokes without their feet touching the bottom of the pool, they were transferred to the swimmers group on another day.

I finally got going at the end of that first summer term and joined the swimmers group at the beginning of the next summer term, in 1938. When you could swim the length of the baths, you were awarded a free pass to use the baths free of charge for a season. I think Mr Briers was quite keen on our learning to swim, for he gave out the free passes and congratulated those who received them at morning assembly, and Mr Briers was not a man much given to congratulations – censure and criticism were more his line.

I think his life was rather difficult during the years that I was at the Big School. He had an invalid wife, whom we hardly ever saw. There was a clever grown-up daughter, Phyllis, who lived away from home doing some kind of high-powered job. When I went to the High School, I saw her name on the Honours Board. She had been awarded a state or county major scholarship sometime in the '20s. In due course my name would be added to the board as a recipient of a county major scholarship in 1948. At that time Phyllis Briers and I were the only alumnae of Rothwell Gladstone Street Council School to feature on the Honours Board, but others may have been added later – I don't know.

But back to the classroom. At the end of our year in Standard One, our class had been together for four years, and there had been very few changes. One girl joined us when she and her little sister moved into Rothwell to live with an auntie after their mother died. Two boys in our class also lost their mothers – I think in childbirth. One of the boys was cared for in his extended family; the other with his siblings and his father moved out of Rothwell.

I remember, too, two other sad little girls from different families whose mothers were in mental homes after childbirth and suffering,

I'm pretty sure, from what today would be recognised and treated as post-natal depression. In those days they were incarcerated for the rest of their lives, and their children were looked after by relatives. Pregnancy and childbirth were still hazardous affairs.

In those days, and in our kind of community, children were more likely to lose a mother than a father. I don't remember anyone losing a father until the war years. The boot and shoe industry, though sometimes monotonous and not well paid, is not dangerous. If we had been a mining or fishing community, it would, of course, have been a different story.

Our class was joined by another girl, Gracie, at some stage during our first year or two or three in the Big School. Gracie's parents were Salvation Army officers, who in those days moved postings every four years. Perhaps they still do. Her dad was a major. I don't remember what rank her mother held, but she had a rank.

Gracie and her two brothers and little sister had special red Sunday jumpers with the words 'Salvation Army' appliquéd in bold gold letters across the front.

This was long before you could get T-shirts printed with any slogan you liked, indeed it was long before any kind of T-shirt appeared in this country.

The rest of us wore jumpers that our mums or grandmas had knitted for us, and Gracie's family's garments seemed to us very exotic. She taught us some of the Salvation Army songs too, and I still remember snatches of two of them:

The devil and me, we don't agree
I hate him, and he hates me
He had me once but he let me go
He wants me again but I will not go
Glory, glory hallelujar (repeated as many times as you liked)

And, sung to a vigorous marching tune:

> Lift up the flag of the blood and the fire
> The yellow, red and blue
> Lift up the Army colours
> I love them, yes I do

It all seemed a lot more fun than the "Gentle Jesus, meek and mild" that was our lot at the Congregational Sunday School.

CHAPTER 13
Preparing for the Scholarship

AT THE END of our year with Miss Tye, those of us who could read fluently and were at home with the four arithmetical mechanical processes went into Standard Three with Miss Rivett. Those who were still struggling went into Standard Two with Miss Hearne. In both cases we joined the corresponding half of the class a year older than us – so I found myself in Standard Three and in the same class as Josie and Heather. We were the scholarship hopefuls and were being fast tracked.

I don't remember a lot about Miss Rivett. She was youngish, college-trained, strict and, I think, a very good teacher. She taught the two halves of the class separately for arithmetic, but together for English. There were new tables to learn: pounds, shillings and pence; yards, feet and inches; stones, pounds and ounces; and others to do with time, liquid measures, longer distances and heavier weights.

And with Miss Rivett, too, we first came across the 'problem people', who tested our ability to apply the mechanical rules to these new tables. The 'problem people' stayed with us for the rest of the Gladstone Street days and, I think, into the first couple of years at the High School. You know the sort of thing: "Wine gums cost a shilling a pound. Mary buys two ounces. How much change does she get from a sixpenny piece?"

Their shopping expeditions grew more complicated, and they made difficult journeys, travelling by different forms of transport at different speeds. Sometimes they did absolutely daft things, like running water into leaking baths. Sometimes they went in for DIY involving linoleum priced by the square yard and paint priced by the quart tin. I was quite fond of the 'problem people'. They were much more interesting than straightforward arithmetic, and my dad absolutely loved them.

At the end of our year with Miss Rivett, we were meant to move up into Standard Four and the tutelage of Mr Tippett. Standard Four had for many years been the responsibility of Mr Playford, an elderly man who had, I think, come up by the pupil teacher route and who was due to retire at the end of the 1939 summer term. Mr Tippett, a college-trainer teacher, would fill Mr Playford's shoes.

However, things did not go entirely according to plan. The second world war began in September 1939 (more of that later), and this delayed the start of the new term and also the arrival of Mr Tippett and meant that Mr Playford stayed for another few weeks, so it was into his hands that we passed in the autumn of 1939. Mr Playford had, I think, spent his whole teaching career at Gladstone Street and was renowned throughout Rothwell as a brilliant history teacher. Grown-ups who had been taught by him as children would say to us when we went up to the 'big' school "You'll have history with Mr Playford. You'll like that." It was spoken without irony, just a simple statement of fact. They had liked history with Mr Playford, everybody did, and we were no exceptions.

Our unlikely and not very suitable class reader was *Little Women*, but Mr Playford placed it in context and filled in the background. We became anti-slavery Unionists to a man and would have followed Abe Lincoln's banners to the ends of the earth.

On another occasion we learned that Mr Playford didn't really hold in with the Norman Conquest. One of his heroes was Hereward the Wake, the Saxon rebel with his followers in their hideout in the middle of the impenetrable marshes near Ely. They would sally forth and harass the Norman invaders, then retreat along the safe paths known only to them back to their base. The Normans tried to follow them but, of course, missed their footing and were sucked down to a horrible, muddy death in the bog. "Served them right", we said, "for being Normans".

In retrospect, I think Mr Playford was a wonderful story-teller rather than a brilliant teacher, but he certainly taught us that the past is a magical country, well worth visiting and learning from – and that is a lesson well worth taking to heart.

Before Christmas, whatever difficulty there had been was sorted out, and Mr Playford was replaced by Mr Tippett, and we continued our inexorable plodding toward the scholarship exam: lots of arithmetic, practice English essays, comprehension tests and other English exercises. When we scholarship hopefuls moved to Mr Briers's care in September 1940, practice intelligence tests were added to our menu, the kind of thing where you complete a pattern or a sequence of pictures or choose the most appropriate word to complete a sentence. They were meant to test innate intelligence but you actually also needed a fair degree of literacy to get through them.

The scholarship exam happened early in March and, like general elections, was always on a Thursday. I can't remember now if it took a whole day or just a morning, but for such a momentous milestone in anyone's life it was surprisingly brief. I found it quite straightforward but was certainly not going to stick out my neck by saying so. I just said, non-committally, that it had been "all right, really".

There was then a period of two or three months marking time, while we waited for the results. We spent some time as a whole class with Mr Tippett. I remember, too, geography lessons with Perce Woolstone, whose main responsibility was the senior boys: those who had not passed the scholarship examination. I was very fond of Perce – he had been a near neighbour for my whole life and was also, you may remember, Mary's and my rescuer from Auntie Hilda's 'shop'. But even Perce could not make scintillating stuff of the countries of Europe and their capitals or the countries of the Empire and their exports. He tried, though.

Then there was Mrs Soars, a widow in charge of the senior girls, Perce's mirror image, so to speak. She taught us singing and had in fact irregularly done so throughout our 'big school' years. It was quite fun. Two classes were squashed together in a classroom and taught the words and tunes of various hymns and folk-songs. Mrs Soars was a strict disciplinarian, quite capable of managing 70 to 80 children without batting an eyebrow.

In the fullness of time, after Mr Briers's poor invalid wife died, he and Mrs Soars got married, as did Perce Woolstone and Miss Rivett, after Perce was demobbed – I think from the RAF – to which he was conscripted soon after I left Gladstone Street. The school had become almost a little marriage bureau. I hope they were all happy. They were good people and deserved to be.

I don't remember any religious instruction at Gladstone Street. As at the infants school, if it happened, it was so negligible that it left no impression. Our morning assemblies, too, were so perfunctory as to be totally immemorable. Mr Briers stood on a chair, told us which hymn we were to sing, Mrs Soars struck up on the piano and we did the best we could. We had no hymn sheets or books and were squashed together standing between desks. I expect Mr Briers then said a prayer, I believe the law required him to. Then he proceeded to the real business: announcements, exhortations, threats and, very occasionally, commendations. Then we dispersed to get on with what we were really there to do.

I don't remember any regular programme of physical education. There was, in any case, no indoor space for it. I seem to recall that Mr Tippett had a penchant for having us marching about rather point-lessly outside. But that was about it.

But, as I said, we were really filling in time between early March and something like mid-May. One morning, a bit before Ro'well Fair Week, Mr Briers called me out of class, took me to his office, told me I had won a scholarship and solemnly shook my hand. Having ascertained that Mum would be in, he sent me home to tell her, with strict injunctions to be sure I was back for afternoon school at 1.30 sharp.

The scholarship covered free tuition at the High School/Grammar School and some further financial support, the details of which I do not remember. Some days later we learned that two other girls and four boys had been awarded 'free' or 'special' places, ie they could attend the High School/Grammar School without paying fees.

Then, a little later on, we learned that two girls had been awarded places at the Central School. These schools were widespread until about the 1960s, usually offering gender-mixed education leading to School Certificate (later O level) plus some vocational education to the age of 16.

So nine of our original class were moving on. This was a *very* good year. The previous year there had been one free place and two Central School places. But then that class had suffered all the disruption of the war starting at the beginning of their scholarship year.

The classmates we left behind were then divided according to gender. All girls over the age of 11 were the responsibility of Mrs Soars, and the boys that of Perce Woolstone and, as I have already indicated, 'life skills' education – cookery, needlework, gardening, woodwork – was added to their curriculum.

There is no doubt that success in the scholarship examination was the first major watershed in my life. If things had gone otherwise, subsequent events would have been entirely different, and I would be writing a very different story.

CHAPTER 14
Lessons out of school

IN THE 1930s children were sent to Sunday School as a matter of course. Unfortunately the Congregational Chapel Sunday School was much the farthest away from Littlewood Street, but that was where we went nevertheless. I found it boring and, in retrospect, it was a cringe-making experience. I can remember as a very young child in the 'babies' section of the Sunday School (run, incidentally, by Miss Harris of the Victoria Infants School) parading around with the other little mites to contribute to the missionary collection, singing

> Do you see this penny? It is brought by me
> For the little children far across the sea.
> Hurry penny, hurry though you are so small.
> Help to tell the children Jesus loves them all.

Ugh!

When we were a little older, we were divided into single-sex groups according to age, each group with a usually very young 'teacher' of the same sex. I don't know what training the teachers were given but it didn't seem to be very effective. The ones I encountered were nice enough girls, well meaning no doubt, but I don't think we learned anything. I remember one in particular, a plump jolly girl with whom we were reading a passage from the Bible, each child reading a verse in turn, saying "If you don't know a word or can't say it, just say 'wheelbarrow' instead".

The start of the second world war disrupted many things, including my Sunday School attendance. When life settled down again after the first few confusing weeks, I didn't go back to Sunday School. I had reached an age when I could be useful at home on Sunday mornings, and my parents respected my reluctance to take part in what seemed to be a pointless exercise.

Piano lessons were not, for me, much more successful than Sunday School. Many homes in those days housed a piano, and adults who could play might offer, for a small sum, to pass on their expertise to children. No training or qualifications were needed or asked for. We had a piano, and Wally could play well. He had a good ear and quickly picked up and rendered any tune he heard. He really hardly needed teaching; it came naturally.

This was not the case with me. I didn't enjoy piano lessons or piano practice and, when something more interesting offered, I was quick off the mark.

Mum became friendly through the St Johns Ambulance Brigade with a young woman, Kathleen Read, who had recently married a Rothwell man and moved into Rothwell. Kathleen was a trained elocution and drama teacher. She wanted to keep her hand in and, presumably, to earn a little extra cash by taking a few pupils. She offered individual or group teaching and, since the piano lessons were not exactly a wild success, my parents thought I might like to switch to elocution. I don't think they could afford both.

Would I? I would indeed! I joined a group of five, Heather, Rita, Kathleen, Pamela and me, and enjoyed it enormously. We all did. Kathleen Read was pretty and lively, enjoyed children and knew how to teach. We did voice production exercises and sometimes giggled at each other's efforts. We learned and recited poems, sometimes individually and sometimes as a group exercise. After a year or two, the elocution lessons came to an end when Kathleen became pregnant. Evening lessons did not marry well with caring for a new baby.

When my parents and Wally moved to London, Mum and Kathleen lost touch for a while, until I got chatting to a young woman, a fellow guest at a party Chris and I were attending. Amazingly, she turned out to be Kathleen's granddaughter! Letters were exchanged, contact was resumed and, when Mum went to Kettering to stay with John and Jenny for a break, Jenny asked Kathleen – still living in Rothwell – and her daughter over.

Mum and Kathleen are both dead now, Kathleen, although the younger by some years, having died first, but I still exchange Christmas cards with Kathleen's daughter Margaret, the baby whose arrival brought the elocution classes to an end.

CHAPTER 15
The war – movement of people

SUNDAY 3 September 1939. The new school year was due to start the next day. It didn't though. The second world war had started instead, and schools were closed for the time being, as were cinemas, swimming-pools and other places where people might congregate. Uncle Irvie and Auntie May had decided that in the event of war May and their young family would be safer in the Forest of Dean than in Rothwell and by implication that I would too.

I don't know what the basis for this decision was, and no one has been able to tell me, but that Sunday afternoon the Groocock family and I were conveyed in Uncle Irvie's car to Mile End. We were quite a houseful. Grandma was living at Fourways, and Rene and Joe had a 16-month-old daughter, Ann, so there we were – five children, three women and Uncle Joe in one small three-bedroomed house. I had a camp bed on the landing. Uncle Irvie, of course, returned to Rothwell – he had a factory to run.

Fortunately, it was a lovely, golden, sunny September, and we were able to spend a lot of time outside. If we had all been cooped up indoors, it would have been a pretty miserable experience. I missed my parents, Wally, Joe and my friends, but I knew my grandma, aunties, uncle and cousins well and had made friends among local children so I was quite content. But there was an air of nervous waiting – something should be happening but wasn't. It was happening in Poland, of course.

About the end of September or beginning of October schools were to re-open, and Tom and I needed to be in school either in Rothwell or in Mile End, so the decision was taken to return to Rothwell.

The government did not share my family's nervousness about the safety of Rothwell. A London elementary school – teachers and pupils – had been evacuated to and billeted in Rothwell. Children of school age were evacuated from the large, vulnerable cities with their schools. Only the youngest children were evacuated with their mothers.

There was a small and not very efficient church school in Rothwell as well as the Victoria Infants School and the Gladstone Street Council School, and the facilities offered by these three now had to be shared with a fourth school. At Gladstone Street, for a while, we boxed and coxed with the London school. One week we did long mornings, 9am to 1pm, and they did long afternoons, 1pm to 5pm, and the next week the positions were reversed. It played hell with dinner-time, I can tell you, with housewives having to provide either a very early or very late dinner for their schoolchildren as well as the usual rushed repast for the factory workers.

Before too long, though, additional facilities were found and pressed into service, mainly assembly rooms belonging to the various churches. My cousin Tom remembers some or all of his infant school years being spent in one of the rooms at the Congregational Chapel instead of at the Victoria Infant School, and Auntie Rene, then living temporarily with us and employed as a teacher at the church school, in fact held her classes in a room attached to the Wesleyan Church. It was all a bit inconvenient, but at least we were now able to follow our usual timetables.

The uncanny quiet of the 'phoney war' period in that first autumn and winter didn't last, of course. After the fall of France and the evacuation of Dunkirk, Hitler put everything into trying to smash the RAF and the south coast towns preparatory to an invasion of England by sea.

One day in September 1940, soon after I had started my 'scholarship' year in Mr Briers's class, there was a letter from Eastbourne in the morning's post. Bob Horsman and Doris and Peggy were having a terrible time (Wilf had already been conscripted), and Bob wrote to ask if we could possibly offer refuge to his wife and daughter.

Of course we could. Mum and Dad had a hurried discussion at dinner-time about what to do, and the upshot was that I was to go to the Post Office on my way back to school to dispatch a telegram saying "RECEIVED LETTER. COME AT ONCE. RUTHWAL." There was some discussion about how to sign the telegram. 'Andrew' seemed a bit cold, but it had to be seen to come from them both. Perhaps the Post Office would accept 'Ruthwal' as one word, thus saving expense. You paid for telegrams by the word. Wally was at school in Kettering, Dad couldn't be late for work to go to the Post Office and for some reason – maybe she had to go to the hospital – Mum couldn't go. So it fell to me.

I was not at all happy. It would make me late for school, something that had never, ever happened before. Mr Briers was very fierce indeed about lateness, and was known to cane persistent latecomers. My parents assured me it would be all right. Mum would write a note, and I could add my own explanation. I was still of an age to believe anything they told me, but I wasn't sure that they knew Mr Briers as well as I did. However, I was a good child and did as I was told.

The Post Office was not on my way back to school; it was quite out of my way. And even if I ran all the way, I would not get to school by 1.30. I did my best. The kind Post Office lady accepted 'Ruthwal' as one word, so there was a penny or two change.

Meanwhile, Mr Briers, marking his register, was perflexed by my absence. Had I been all right at the end of morning school? Yes. Had I said anything to anyone about not being there this afternoon? No. Had anyone who came to school by the same route that I used seen me? No. He went to the senior girls' class to ask my cousin Mary if she could throw any light on the situation. No. Had any of the senior girls en route for school seen me? Yes! Two girls from the other end of the town, returning for afternoon school, had seen me 'down street', running the *wrong way*, ie *away* from school.

When I arrived back at school, panting and not more than about 10 minutes late, Mr Briers was in the corridor talking to Mr Tippett at the doorway of Mr Tippett's classroom. I think they were talking about me, because one of them said "There you are!" or "Here she is!" or something like that. I gave Mum's note to Mr Briers and answered a few supplementary questions. My parents had been right. He was not cross at all. He asked if I had managed all right at the Post Office, said I was 'a good girl', patted me on the shoulder and escorted me into our classroom to make a belated start on our English lesson.

My classmates, of course, were agog but they had to wait, as I had to wait for their graphic accounts of the questioning about my non-appearance at registration. In Mr Briers's shoes, I would have told them what had happened, and I would also have gone into the senior girls' class to tell Mary that I was all right. But this was 1940, and he had done pretty well by the standards of his time.

My schoolmates had to wait till afternoon playtime when, for the first and only time in my school life, I was the centre of playground attention. They were disappointed that it had, after all, been a parent-sanctioned, Mr Briers-approved non-adventure. I had not been running away from home or escaping from kidnappers. And Mary was pretty miffed with me for a day or two. She thought she should have been in the picture.

My mother, never one to let the grass grow under her feet, had already worked out by tea-time what adjustments to our living arrangements would be needed. Wally would move into my single bedroom. His double bedroom would be taken over by Doris and Peggy, and I would sleep in my parents' room on a small single bed that converted from a large wooden armchair we had.

Moving a child's bedroom in those days was not a major operation. It was just a matter of changing the bed linen and moving a few clothes from one cupboard to another. Today it would probably be several days' work, with all the electronic equipment and homework facilities and so forth to be relocated. We did it that evening and put the new arrangements into operation that night. Dad had managed to scrounge a sturdy cardboard box from the factory and adapted it to make a bed for Chum. With a piece of old blanket for lining, it looked quite comfortable, and we put it under the cupboard that the wireless stood on. They would not, of course, be able to bring his basket with them.

The Horsmans didn't let the grass grow either: when I got home from school the next afternoon, they were already there – Doris, Bob, Peggy and Chum. Bob had been allowed – or perhaps had just taken – a day off work to see his wife and daughter safely through the chaos of wartime travelling, but he had to be back in Eastbourne for work next morning so, after a quick snack and a cup of tea, he was on his way.

After tea, Joe returned from his day's activities. Chum set up an excited yapping and made darts forward from where he had been sitting near Doris's ankles. Joe stood still in his usual 'What can I do for you, then?' mode. Chum, nonplussed, subsided, backed away and took up his position by Doris's ankles again, occasionally growling unconvincingly. Joe then proceeded to his usual place on the hearthrug and settled down comfortably. They never became friends but they tolerated each other, and there was never any doubt as to who was top animal.

We adapted to the change in our lives fairly easily. It was hardest, of course, for Mum and Doris, but they managed pretty well. Peggy, now a pretty and lively 17-year-old, had worked in a shop in Eastbourne and had no difficulty finding a place as a shop assistant at Timothy White's in Kettering. I enjoyed the novelty of her big sisterly presence in our home.

A few weeks later, when the evenings were drawing in and getting chilly, Bob suddenly turned up unannounced. His workplace (I am not sure what he did) had been destroyed, and I think no 90 Sidney

Road had been damaged too, so he had decided to up sticks and join the rest of the family. Poor old Peggy had to transfer to a makeshift bed in the front room downstairs, and we were really beginning to be rather overcrowded and under each other's feet.

Bob said he would look for a job, then look for somewhere suitable for them to live as it looked as though they would not be going back to Eastbourne any time soon. He was as good as his word. The boot and shoe factories were working all out now, even with overtime working, and, though their work was rated to be 'of national importance', boot and shoe work was not a 'reserved occupation' like mining or farming, so the young workers were being conscripted, and the factory owners were looking to recruit new blood.

The grim truth is that every serviceman killed or captured meant a full set of uniform and kit, including boots, lost. Our comparative prosperity in wartime rested on those young, broken lives. So Bob went into a shoe factory and managed to rent part of a house on the other side of town. The house was being bought by a young couple, but the husband had been conscripted , and the young wife was glad of help with the mortgage and the bills. The Horsmans moved out of Littlewood Street just before Christmas and, in fact, settled in Northamptonshire. They never did go back to Eastbourne.

Peggy met and married a young man from Broughton, a small town on the other side of Kettering, and settled there to raise a family. Bob and Doris, too, bought a small house in Broughton to be near their daughter and family, and there they ended their days. After the move we did not see a lot of them – it was an awkward journey by public transport – but we kept in touch.

In 1980 my dad, now in failing health, reached his 80th birthday, and we organised a family party for him at our house in Fulham. We invited Bob; Doris by then was very frail and unable to travel and perhaps not well enough even to leave with Peggy and family, so we didn't tell Dad that Bob might be coming, as we didn't want him to be disappointed. In the event it worked out, and John and Jenny were able to bring Bob with them. Bob and Dad's final reunion was quite a tear-jerker; they had not counted on seeing each other again.

Back in 1940 a lot of people, who had never expected they would need to move, were having to relocate. I have mentioned the evacuees: the official ones, government organised, like the London children who shared our school buildings, and private ones like the Horsmans who made their own arrangements with family or friends in 'safe' areas. I knew quite a few of these private evacuees both in Rothwell and at the High School in Kettering.

Then there was conscription. Fit young men over the age of 18 were directed into the armed forces, and young unmarried women were also directed into work of national importance or into the armed forces. As it happened, our family was less affected by conscription than many. Dad and Charlie were too old and Wally was not physically fit.

Uncle John and Uncle Tom were both in reserved occupations: John working for the gas board, and Tom making aeroplanes at Filton in Bristol. Uncle Len was conscripted, but he was, in fact, granted long spells of compassionate leave because of the illness and deaths of his wife and child.

Uncle Joe was our main active participant in the war, despite being slightly lame as a result of a childhood illness. He was 'called up' in May 1940 and joined the Royal Electrical and Mechanical Engineers (REME). He was moved to various army camps all over England but eventually ended up at Warminster.

He and Auntie Rene decided that they would rent out Fourways and that Rene and Ann would take lodgings near Warminster so that they could all be together as much as possible. Grandma moved to Rothwell and stayed with Auntie May and family for the duration of the war – a rock and stay to us all.

Towards the end of 1943, Joe was given embarkation leave before being sent overseas, and Rene and Ann were able to spend his leave with him. Then they came to us at Littlewood Street. So another reorganisation. Wally moved back to the single room, and Rene and Ann and I occupied his double room, Ann in the same convertible bed I had used in 1940. John had just been born (I have already told you what a poorly baby he was at first), and Mum was not well, so it was great to have Auntie Rene and Ann with us.

Joe was sent to North Africa and then to the Sicily landings and the advance through Italy. When he eventually returned, he brought us all presents from Italy and stories of his experiences.

As I have already mentioned, once we had all sorted ourselves out and settled down and Mum and John were in better health, Auntie Rene took up a post at the Church School teaching children with learning difficulties. It was not an easy assignment. Her classroom was not purpose built, and the equipment and teaching materials were sketchy to say the least, but she always spoke of her pupils with affection and humour. They were lucky children to have her.

Uncle Joe was eventually demobbed but before things were properly sorted out at Mile End, Auntie Rene fell ill with tuberculosis and stayed with us so that my mother could nurse her back to health, which she did very skilfully. Grandma went back to Mile End to look after Uncle Joe, who resumed his duties in the family business, and I went for two or three weeks in the summer to give Grandma a hand and to keep her company. My cousin Tom, I think, also went to Mile End for a while that summer holiday with the same remit.

I remember well that during that stay I tasted fresh salmon for the first time. Uncle Joe had managed to buy a piece of Wye salmon, and Grandma poached it for Sunday dinner – a revelation!

Throughout the war young men from all the combatant countries, of course, were being conscripted into the armed forces and transported to wherever national need dictated. After the Japanese bombing of Pearl Harbor in December 1941, the United States of

America declared war on Japan and Germany, and young American recruits – GIs – began to arrive in Britain.

There was an American Air Force base at Harrington, only a couple of miles from Rothwell, and two or three others in the vicinity. Black and white Americans were strictly segregated and not allowed to visit the same towns when they had time off, though, as I have already told you, necessity sometimes dictated that they ended up wounded in the same hospital.

Young American airmen sometimes spent time in Rothwell, particularly at dances organised as money raisers by local organisations. On the whole, youngish Englishmen – forces personnel on leave, men in reserved occupations, soldiers from a training establishment at Rushton – regarded the Americans with suspicion and resentment. It was said that they were "over paid, over sexed and over here", and occasionally there would be a bit of a rough-house.

Cheeky children regarded them as a source of largesse. "Got any gum, chum?" was a frequently heard request, which more often than not met with a positive response. Young women, whose boyfriends or husbands had been conscripted, often regarded them with a favourable eye: they had smart uniforms and money to spend. There were a few babies born out of wedlock, and one or two marriages. After the war ended, there were special transports of 'GI brides' to the USA. The rest of us regarded them more or less benevolently. After all, they were youngsters far from home and not by their own choice. We were encouraged by the authorities to fraternise, and the GIs were similarly encouraged to make friends.

Many families, including ours, 'adopted' a young American for a while. Our American was called Larry, and I can't remember how we came by him but he was often at our house in 1944. He was a pleasant, quietly spoken young man, an air force photographer. The informal snapshots of our family from this period were all taken by Larry – photographic film was not available to British civilians.

To encourage such liaisons, the Americans could buy in their camp canteens various items to take as gifts to augment the rations of their hosts. I remember particularly big tins of fruit cocktail. We had been able to buy tinned fruit salad, containing large lumps of mixed fruit in syrup – before the war, but this delicate macedoine of fruits seemed infinitely more sophisticated and attractive.

The other item I remember is big tins of sausage meat, the meat being surrounded by a copious amount of pure pork fat. We used the fat to make a rich pastry and the sausage meat to make a pie filling. I think we would find it too rich and heavy today, but in those lean times it went down a treat. Larry also brought chocolate and occasionally oranges.

Then, early in 1945, he disappeared. There was no way we could find out what had happened to him and, in the end, we assumed sadly that he had probably been killed in action. There were heavy bombing raids of Germany at this time. Sometimes, in the early morning, the still-dark sky would be filled with scores of bombers, flying in formation, their red landing lights already glowing. And sometimes there were a few, not in formation, struggling back wounded. We crossed our fingers and hoped they would make it, but our Larry may have been in one that didn't.

The only other foreigners I met as a result of the war were two young Italians who had been brought to Britain as prisoners of war and were employed as farm workers. Audrey Grey, my friend and schoolmate from our first day at the Victoria Infants School through to the sixth form at Kettering High School, was a farmer's daughter. Audrey and her family lived at Manor Farm in Orton, a hamlet about a mile from Rothwell, and we were frequent visitors to each other's homes during childhood and adolescence.

It was at Manor Farm that I met Jean and Murro (I write their names phonetically – I never saw them written down). I don't know what their status was. They came as prisoners of war, probably taken in North Africa in 1942 or early '43. In September 1943 Italy surrendered, so presumably Jean and Murro became neutrals. Then, when Italy declared war on Germany in October 1943, presumably they became allies. It must have been very confusing for them.

Anyway, Farmer Grey was very pleased with them. They had a large room over one of the outbuildings and were delighted to show it to me when Audrey asked them. It was very neat and clean, and I'm sure they did their own cooking. I had never seen a crucifix and holy pictures in a domestic setting before, and I had never encountered a language barrier before. I found it very frustrating. There were so many things I would have liked to ask them. Communication problems of this kind have beset and bedevilled me all my life and still do.

CHAPTER 16
The war – air raid precautions

NO ONE KNEW what to expect of the war but, given the experience of the Spanish Civil War, it was pretty certain that there would be bombing of the civilian population. It was thought quite possible that gas would be used too. I don't remember exactly when we were issued with gas masks, but they were fitted by council employees who brought them round and fitted them at home.

There were special red rubber Mickey Mouse masks for young children, but I was big enough now to have the ordinary black rubber version like the rest of the family. They were held on by straps that had to be correctly adjusted, and that is what the council people did. Each mask fitted into a special cardboard box but pretty soon you were able to get lighter, more portable gas mask carriers, as we were meant to take them everywhere.

If you turned up at school without your mask, you had to go home to get it, but you wouldn't use this as a skive to get out of school. You had to get permission from Mr Briers himself, and he got very cross with people who forgot their gas masks – and incandescent if it happened again.

During the first year of the war, Mr Tippett used to test our masks from time to time. We had to put them on, and he would hold a thin piece of card over the nozzle of each child's mask in turn and tell the testee to breathe in. If the card stuck to the nozzle, the mask was all right. If not, Mr Tippett fiddled with the straps until he got the desired result. You could make very satisfactory rude noises with a gas mask, but it wasn't a good idea to do that in school.

I don't remember when we stopped carrying the masks. There were no gas attacks, and gradually the practice of carrying the masks fell into disuse and was finally abandoned.

There were bombing raids though, especially in 1940 and 1941.

The factory buzzers were silenced for the duration of the war, because the warning that enemy planes were in the vicinity was the wailing of a siren on a rising and falling note. The 'all clear', denoting that danger was over, was a steady note. Church bells were silenced too. They were to be rung only in the event of an enemy invasion, a very real possibility in 1940.

Some people had air raid shelters made. Uncle Irvie had one dug in his garden and, at first, when the air raid warning sounded, we would get up and go round to Rushton Road and join the Groococks in the shelter. After a while, the nights got colder and the shelter got damper, and it became fairly clear that the German bombers were passing overhead on their way to more important targets, so we stayed in our beds. Quite often I didn't even wake up when the siren sounded.

I think only once in the course of the war did any bombs drop on Rothwell. A few incendiary bombs fell harmlessly on the middle of a road, probably jettisoned by a bomber on its way home rather than dropped with intent.

Above-ground brick shelters were also built, including two in the school gardens at Gladstone Street. Once or twice we had a practice air raid drill – getting out of the school building and into the shelter in a quick and orderly fashion – but we never had to do it for real. There were similar shelters at Kettering High School, but I don't remember any air raid drills.

Probably, like the carrying of gas masks, the practice fell into abeyance. We were each required, though, to have a haversack to take to the shelter if need be. The haversack was supposed to contain a bottle of water, some biscuits, some dried fruit, a torch and probably a few other things as well. Eventually the biscuits and raisins got eaten, the water got stale, the torch batteries failed and, fortunate beings that we were, we never had need of them.

My dad was an air raid warden. His wardens' post was an empty shop half way down Ragsdale Street, where he would join three or four other wardens and two teenage boys who were messengers. I remember that the first Christmas these boys solemnly gave each of their wardens a rather sweet traditional Christmas card inscribed "From your loving messengers".

If there had been a real air raid, the wardens' work would have been vital and dangerous but, in the event, they chatted and listened to the wireless, checked the stirrup pump and fire buckets, drank tea and waited for the 'all clear'. Their main function in Rothwell was to see that the blackout was observed , and this was done rigorously. It was illegal to show any light at all after the published black out time. You had to buy thick black material to make curtains or cover your windows in other ways.

My dad, with his usual competence and thoroughness, made light-weight portable shutters for our downstairs windows. They were made of several thicknesses of brown paper on a light wooden frame and were made exactly to measure and could be slotted into place in an instant by anyone with an adequate arm span. You were allowed to use a torch or bicycle lamp outdoors, but had to cover the glass with tissue paper or gauze to filter the light. There were quite a few accidents because of the blackout.

Mum, as a member of the St John's Ambulance Brigade, would be needed if there were air raid casualties, and there was a big A outside our front door. Quite superfluous really; everybody in the streets around us knew where to come for first aid. Both my parents had tin hats and took them very seriously. We were not allowed to meddle with them or try them on for fun.

The tin hats, though, like the gas masks and the air-raid-shelter haversacks, were not destined to be used in earnest.

CHAPTER 17
The war as a leveller

WHEN WE KNEW that I was going to the High School, we did what we would have done anyway, war or no war. One evening after tea, Mum and I went to visit a family we knew whose daughter was taking her School Certificate in the summer of 1941 and was to leave school afterwards.

For a working class family, kitting out a child for High School or Grammar School had always been a major financial headache. A full uniform and all manner of equipment were required, so it often happened that a school starter and a school leaver would match themselves up and a mutually advantageous exchange would take place.

We came away with a hockey stick, a tennis racquet with press and waterproof cover, a hatband and probably other bits and pieces too. Our friend, on the other hand, had a small sum to help fit her up for life as an office worker. The difference was that nearly everyone was at it now. In that grim summer of 1941 there was precious little in the way of raw materials or productive capacity to spare for fripperies like hockey sticks or geometry sets or hatbands. You got what you could where you could.

Second-hand goods, hand-me-downs and remaindered stock no longer indicated a shortage of funds.

When the 1941 High School intake assembled that autumn, by no means everyone had managed to get it all together. I remember one girl in my form wore a red knitted jumper-suit for several weeks before the gym tunic her parents ordered arrived.

Then there was rationing from the beginning of 1940. Basic foodstuffs – butter, margarine, cheese, bacon, tea, sugar – were rationed by weight, eggs by number, meat by price. You could have a miniscule piece of steak or a much greater weight of shin of beef or belly pork: it was up to you and your culinary skills.

The meat ration also later included two-penn'orth of corned beef per head. It came in long tins, which were opened by the butcher and cut according to the number of ration books presented. Even baby John was entitled to his two-penn'orth of corned beef, and the one shilling and two-penn'orth that we got on seven ration books was enough for a hash or a shepherd's pie or a good pile of sandwiches.

Offal and sausages were not rationed, but the supply was erratic and sparse. Poultry and game were not rationed, and boys still brought rabbits round to the back door. Vegetarians (much rarer in the 1940s than they are today) could forgo their meat ration and get extra cheese instead. Some families registered one member as a vegetarian, as this suited them better.

Ration books came in various colours. Green for pregnant women, nursing mothers and the under-fives, who had first choice of fruit, a daily pint of milk and a double supply of eggs. They were also entitled to concentrated orange juice and cod liver oil and sometimes other extras. Blue books were for five to 16-year-olds. They got the full meat ration, half a pint of milk a day and fresh oranges on the very rare occasions that they were available.

Adults had buff-coloured books, and there was an ingenious points system to allocate foods in short supply but not in universal demand – tinned foods, dried fruit, some kinds of biscuits, some kinds of cereals, jams and marmalade and various others. Each item had a certain points value, and whether you spent your points on tinned peaches or grapenuts or Spam or raisins was up to you.

Rations and points value varied from time to time, but were the same for everybody. Clothing was also rationed. You had a certain number of clothing coupons, with an extra allowance for growing children. Shopkeepers displayed items of clothing or fabrics with their coupon value as well as their price, though there was often not much to display. You could spend your clothing coupons anywhere, but for your food you had to be registered with a particular retailer. We, of course, were registered with the Co-op.

Fresh fish was not rationed: the supply was too rare and erratic for it to be practicable. If Mr Munton had fish, there was a huge queue, both for wet fish and for fish and chips. When there was no fish, he cooked 'scallops' – thin slices of potato dipped in batter and fried as for fish – and very palatable they were too, with salt and vinegar.

Petrol was also in very short supply and only available to people who needed it for work: farmers, delivery men and so forth. There was little or none for private motoring, and most private motorists (there were not many) put their cars in store for the duration.

The point of all this is that the rationing system was a great equaliser. Of course, there were some evasions, some 'black market' transactions, and the wealthy could eat out at restaurants, some of which continued to function, but by and large everyone was bound by the same regulations.

Having said that, though, I am well aware that country dwellers like us were much better placed than townsfolk. We had our vegetables. We had our wild food, including rabbits. People were allowed to keep a limited number of chickens. Uncle Irvie did. Heather's dad did. Grandpa kept tame rabbits for the pot. I remember after the war being surprised to learn that there was a serious shortage of onions in towns, onions having been imported from Spain and France before the war. I have never lacked an onion in my life.

Incidentally, the economic damage done by the war was such that some rationing continued for nine years after hostilities ended. My son Frank, born in January 1954, had a ration book for the first six months of his life, though only tea and meat were still rationed then.

Because of food shortages and shortages in general, there were vigorous government campaigns to encourage economy, self-sufficiency and recycling. Newspapers were thin and fragile, but they were an important vehicle for government campaigns, as were posters and leaflets.

Cartoon characters, such as Potato Pete and Dr Carrot urged us to Dig for Victory, and Food Facts columns in the papers advised how to make the most of what was available, including the famous Woolton Pie named after the Minister for Food, Lord Woolton. The pie filling was assorted vegetables, which were covered by a potato crust.

Mrs Sew and Sew advised us how to 'make do and mend' – children's clothes from the best parts of outworn adult clothes, handkerchiefs and tea-towels from worn-out sheets and so on. But people like us knew about that already.

Someone once said of my generation – born at the depth of the Depression, reared and grown to adulthood through the war years and the years of post-war austerity – "You can recognise us. We always clear our plates, we make do and mend, and we save bits of string." I certainly run true to type.

My bred-in-the-bone frugality has survived the throw-away society of the later 20th and early 21st centuries and arrived ready for the depression of the late 'noughties'. We don't waste food in this house. Every last bacon rind or spring onion top or parsley stalk is destined for the stock pot.

If something gets broken or damaged, my instinct is to reach for the sticky tape or glue or a needle and thread, rather than bin it and head out to buy a new one, and we have a truly magnificent collection of bits of string, some of them going back decades. Such is the legacy of the 1930s and '40s.

Government campaigns also enjoined us to watch our tongues and not to inadvertently let slip any information that might be of value to the enemy. Posters and newspaper advertisements proclaimed 'Walls have ears', 'Careless talk costs lives', 'Be like Dad, keep Mum' (a bit dubious that one, 70 years on). This all sounds melodramatic today, but in 1940 and 1941, when invasion was on the cards, it made sense.

Signposts were removed and place names painted over at railway stations to confuse an invading army. We were all issued with identity cards in 1940. I don't remember how they were issued, but I remember our numbers. The first seven digits of our family's numbers were the same: RJKD316 for the four of us. Only the last digit was different – 1 for Dad, 2 for Mum, 3 for Wally and 4 for me. Apparently the number indicated where we lived and our place in the household. When John was born in 1943, I expected his identity number to be RJKD3165, but it was something quite different.

We were supposed to carry our identity cards always, like our gas masks, and a number of urban myths circulated about over-officious policemen and air raid wardens sending people who had forgotten to carry their cards to report to police stations, but I never knew anyone to whom this had happened.

A thriving little industry grew up producing identity bracelets with name and number engraved. Jewellers made rather smart ones, but a proletarian version could be obtained from Woolworths. You had to present your identity card to have one made. The High School waived its 'no jewellery' rule to allow identity bracelets. Previously only wrist watches had been excepted.

CHAPTER 18
The end of the war

1940 AND 1941 were bleak years. I was a child and was protected, but I knew that anxiety was in the air. The summer of 1940 was particularly tense, with the Dunkirk evacuation and the Battle of Britain, which precipitated the Horsman family's joining us in Rothwell. In June 1941 Hitler invaded the Soviet Union and by the end of the year was within 25 miles of Moscow. It is not my business nor my intention to write a history of the second world war but only to record its repercussions on my life and on the many other lives that touched mine.

During 1942 the atmosphere changed. The Soviet Union was holding on and the United States had entered the war after the Japanese attack on Pearl Harbor. The Battle of the Atlantic – U-boat attacks on convoys carrying food and other supplies from the USA to Britain – continued to endanger our rations, but progress was being made in decoding messages the Germans sent to their U-boats.

By 1943 the mood began to be cautiously upbeat as the German armies were driven back in the Soviet Union, and British and American troops were victorious in North Africa and landed in Italy. We were now exhorted to invest our spare cash in National Savings, for the war was hideously expensive in every way. By the time of the D-Day landings on the Normandy coast in June 1944, it was clearly only a matter of time, though it was nearly another year before the allied armies converged on Berlin, Hitler committed suicide and Germany surrendered. This was on 7 May 1945, but the official announcement was delayed until 8 May so that it could be made simultaneously in London, Moscow and Washington.

That day and 9 May were public holidays. We had a street party but I don't remember whether it was on the 8th or 9th. The weather was a bit dodgy, so the party was held in a large room at the Avalon factory. Every household contributed something: corned beef sandwiches, Spam sandwiches, scrambled dried egg sandwiches, jam tarts – whatever you could manage. We took along some sausage rolls.

In the evening there were some rather disorganised jollifications in the town, and an interdenominational open-air thanksgiving service was held in the Mounts park the following Sunday. The first of the two days holiday, 8 May, was of course VE Day, Victory in Europe Day. The war in the far east continued until August.

That summer, after Auntie Rene's and my school terms ended, we set off on a little trip together. We were both keen to visit Canterbury and decided to walk the Pilgrims' Way from London. I don't remember whereabouts on the edge of London we began our adventure, but it took several days, and we found bed and breakfast accommodation along the way.

We enjoyed Canterbury, then decided to take a train or bus to Dover to see the sea – beaches had been forbidden territory during the war, but now there was free access again. It was a lovely day, and the beach was crowded. It was 6 August, and it was there that we learned about Hiroshima. We were back in Rothwell when the second atom bomb was dropped on Nagasaki on 9 August, and Japan surrendered on 14 August. The next day was VJ Day. I don't remember any celebrations, though I expect there were some. We were glad the war was over, of course, but the manner of its ending was profoundly shocking. Sixty six years on, it is still profoundly shocking. It always will be.

CHAPTER 19
Kettering High School

I BECAME a Kettering High School girl one day early in September 1941. The High School first opened its doors in 1913. The Balfour Education Act of 1902 made county councils responsible for secondary (grammar and high) schools, which would be partly supported by the rates, though they would also be able to charge fees. However, a number of scholarships and 'special places' were to be awarded to 11-year-olds from local elementary schools who acquitted themselves well in the 'scholarship' examination. And that, of course, as I have already explained, is how I came to be a High School girl.

The Conservative-controlled Northamptonshire County Council rather dragged its feet in following up the 1902 Act. It was probably reluctant to put an extra burden on the rates paid by the many farmers and landowners in the county, and it engaged in lengthy financial wrangling with the trustees of the ancient endowed Kettering Grammar School for boys that was to be subsumed into the new county school.

At last a building to house both the High School and the Grammar School was commissioned and built in Bowling Green Road. The construction cost was £13,575, and the architects' fees amounted to £536 13s. A whole new building for £14,111 13s! And a handsome building it was too, built in neo-Georgian style and standing three storeys high. Early photographs show it fronted with heavy iron railings and double gates but, by the time I arrived, these had been requisitioned for munitions.

Splendid though the building was, careful economies had been observed in the internal provisions. The High School was housed at one end and the Grammar School at the other, but in between was shared territory. A two-storey high assembly hall, which doubled as a gymnasium, had to be shared, as did the library, art room and laboratories, which were all in this central section. On the third floor was the kitchen, which provided school dinners for both schools, and the dining room where they were eaten was next door. When not in use for dining, this room doubled as a music room.

You might be excused for thinking that the middle of the top floor was not the most sensible place to put a kitchen requiring delivery of quantities of heavy provisions and generating a fair amount of waste, but I suspect that the architects who submitted the design and the county councilors who accepted it didn't have that much hands-on experience of kitchens.

By 1941 both school populations had grown considerably, and both now had supplementary accommodation known as 'huts' in the playgrounds. Our hut contained two classrooms with a lobby for hanging coats and other things in between. In each of the classrooms was an iron stove which had to be fed with coke by an assistant school-keeper at dinner time. The stove was surrounded by a sturdy fence with lockable gate; it looked rather like an outsize playpen. If your desk was near the stove, it could get uncomfortably hot, while the far corners of the room got rather chilly. The year that my form was housed in one of the hut rooms, we wanted to roast chestnuts on the stove but never managed to work out a satisfactory method.

I was rather more apprehensive about the High School than I had been about the Victoria Infants School seven years previously. We had been sent an awful lot of material from the school, despite wartime paper shortages. A great many items still seemed to be required – how was I ever going to be able to keep track of them all?

And there was a formidable list of school rules – there seemed to be an awful lot of ways you could upset the authorities, either by doing something you shouldn't, like running in a corridor, or not doing something you should, like wearing your school hat in the street. Heather, a year older then me, had entered the High School the previous year and did her best to reassure me.

That first morning, Heather and I walked down to the bus stop together, as we would do for many mornings to come. At the bus stop we met Audrey and June, the other two girls from Gladstone Street who were also starting at the High School. We fervently hoped that we would all three be placed in the same form. The bus began its journey in Desborough, so there was quite a contingent of High School girls on it already when it stopped to pick up the Rothwell travelers. It was not a dedicated school bus; members of the public used it too.

Our school day began at 10.30am. I accepted then that this was the way things were but, with a lifetime's experience behind me, it now seems to me an incomprehensible arrangement. A prestigious London girls school, Dame Alice Owen School, had been evacuated to Kettering and shared with us the High School end of the building. Their school day ran from 8am to 10.15am with a long break until it resumed from 3.45pm to 5.30pm. Ours ran from 10.30am to 3.30pm with an hour's break for dinner. Who on earth can have proposed and who can have accepted such an unreasonable sharing?

But that's how it was, and that's how it went on until the end, or almost the end, of the war. I don't remember the details exactly. After our first year, on some mornings we had an 'early' lesson starting at 9.30 at one of several sites in Kettering, but the short school day meant a heavy burden of homework and no after-school activities.

Anyway, at 10.30 we arrived at school by the back door. The front door was for visitors, teaching staff and the sixth form. Just inside the back door was the cloakroom, in which we would later be allocated places, and indoor lavatories, washhand basins and roller-towels, luxuries to which Audrey, June and I were unaccustomed at Gladstone Street and Victoria Infants.

For the moment we went straight to the assembly hall. After a fairly short, brisk morning assembly, form lists were read. There was a preparatory school attached to the High School. It was, in essence, a private school catering for girls from the age of eight. The prep school was based in a separate building, a large, converted private house called Hillside, a few minutes' walk from the main school. The High School's headmistress also ran the prep school and had an apartment at Hillside: a sort of 'tied cottage', I suppose.

There were three forms at Hillside: Forms I, II B and II A, so the main High School started with form III, and there were three third forms: III P, Q and R (Roman numerals were always used to designate the forms). To our great relief, Audrey, June and I were in the same form, III Q. I think, as far as possible, girls from the same elementary school were placed together. All the Desborough girls were in our form too. The 20 or so girls from Hillside were divided between the three forms.

The first day we spent with our form teacher, Miss Mitchell, getting organised. We were each allocated a desk with lift-up lid, where we kept all our books and other paraphernalia. I don't know what the Dame Alice Owen girls did with their equipment, but our desks were certainly our territory.

We were also allocated a cloakroom locker – a misnomer as it didn't lock. It was a long, open cubby hole with two pegs in it and a shoe rack underneath. You left your outdoor clothes and shoes here, and your slipper bag was hung on one of the pegs. I had never had a slipper bag before – I don't think most of us had – but the school rules were very clear about it. It had to be made from a piece of red twill of designated size, available from a certain shop in Kettering which also did blazer badges and hatbands when these were available.

Miraculously, the shop had had a supply of red twill adequate for the needs on the 1941 intake and in good time for the slipper bags to be made. The owner's name had to be embroidered in white on the bag, so it was essentially a homemade job. We had no problem with that: my dad wrote my name in pencil very carefully on the piece of twill, and I embroidered it myself. Thanks to Miss Tye, I could do a very neat chain stitch. Then Mum stitched up the sides on the sewing-machine and made a hem at the top, we put a tape through the hem, and there we were!

I think in those days most households were probably capable of running up a slipper bag. The bag was meant to contain gym shoes, indoor shoes and gym kit, ie a pair of black sateen knickers and a green lock-knit cotton top. My bag lacked the green top, as did many others. Supplies were awaited. In the mean time, we did gym in our vests.

The slipper bag stayed in school for the whole term. Incredible as it now seems, no one took their bag and kit home to be washed until the beginning of the next holiday.

Everything had to be marked with its owner's name. Before the war, Cash's name tapes were used by those who could afford them, but now they were not always available, and many people resorted to marking ink and ordinary white tape. We would have done that anyway – another wartime social leveller.

Most of the county secondary schools created under the 1902 Act copied many of the traditions and much of the ethos of public schools, and Kettering High School was no exception. We had a uniform, we had prefects, a Head Girl and a Deputy Head Girl, a house system and a broadly similar curriculum. But there were significant differences. Our house system, for instance, was purely competitive.

In both the public schools and the London comprehensives that I came to know from the 1950s and '60s onwards, there was a strong pastoral element in the house system, with the teaching staff actively involved. At Kettering High School the house system was run entirely by sixth form girls, and competition on the sports field and particularly in the examination hall was fierce.

Audrey and I were placed in St Andrew's House; June, I think, was in St George's, and Heather was in St Patrick's. There was also a St David's. You had to sew a piece of coloured ribbon on your gym tunic to show which house you were in. In one respect at least we differed from many county secondary schools: we were placed in mixed ability forms. Most secondary schools with more than one form intake streamed their pupils in those days. Kettering High School didn't, though Kettering Grammar School did.

This sounds fine and progressive, as I'm sure the intentions were, but mixed ability teaching methods were not used in the mixed ability classrooms. Most teachers, I'm afraid, taught to the top of the ability range, which was great if that was where you found yourself, as I did. But it was pretty dull going if you were in the middle and dire if you were at the bottom end.

At the end of the school year, examinations in all academic subjects were set and taken by all the pupils in a year group – 93 girls, I think, in my year – and in each subject pupils were ranked from first to 93rd. After the exams, the whole year group assembled in the library, and Miss Whyte, the headmistress, read the mark list for each subject. There were half a dozen or so of us who were at or near the top of each list, and we eagerly awaited our placings and found the whole thing exciting.

It was probably not at all exciting to wait and see if you were 49th or 53rd or 60th, and must have been quite stomach-churningly dreadful to wonder if you were going to be at the very end of the list or one or two from the bottom, for the lists bore an awful similarity. That was not the end though. Somebody had the unenviable job of averaging out each girl's marks across the whole range of subjects, and at the final school assembly Miss Whyte read out the rankings for each year group.

It does not surprise me now that this system resulted in a huge amount of wastage.

As soon as the statutory leaving age – then 14 – was reached, far too many girls left the High School and went to work, usually in offices. I can remember the names of all but three or four of the girls in my form, and I can reliably remember that 12 of them left at the end of our third year, ie as soon as they could. Four of the girls who had joined us from Hillside had been sent by their parents to boarding schools at the age of 12 or 13, so we were reduced to something like half of the original intake – not a good record.

At the end of our third year (Upper IV), we were reduced to two forms (Lower V R and Lower V P) and began on our two-year School Certificate course. The School Certificate was a precursor of O levels and later GCSEs, taken usually at the age of 16. It was rather more prescriptive in its demands than its successors, and results were graded in four categories: very good, credit, pass and fail. To be awarded a certificate, you had to get at least a pass grade in five subjects, which had to include English language, maths and a language other than English.

We were in the Upper V when we took our School Certificate, and those who were successful could, if they wished, enter the VI form and begin a Higher School Certificate course – but more of that later.

By 1941 the ban on married women teachers had been lifted, and there was one married teacher on the High School staff, Mrs Huggett who taught French. Several years later another married teacher, Mrs Cousins who taught gymnastics and games, joined us. There were no others in my time.

Another feature of war-time schools was that there were no young, newly qualified teachers. Young women as well as young men were required for the war effort. Our staff, then, was composed of women in their 30s, 40s and 50s, and all the teachers of academic subjects were graduates. That may sound a bit grim but, in fact, it wasn't. These women, born at the end of the 19th or near the beginning of the 20th centuries must have come from comfortably-off families, for university educations did not come cheap in those days, and there was not much support for less prosperous students – but they came from families who thought it was worth educating their girls, not a widely held attitude in those days when female graduates would usually have to retire from employment if they got married.

The family of Lord Redesdale portrayed in her novels by his eldest daughter, Nancy Mitford, was typical of the time. Tom, the son, was sent to Eton: the six girls, two of them very clever indeed, were under-educated at home.

It is one of my unprovable contentions that female graduates in the first part of the 20th century were more likely to be politically progressive than their male counterparts.

Our headmistress was Miss Janet Whyte, classicist, graduate of Newnham College, Cambridge, reportedly former suffragette, though of the non-militant tendency. In those days heads seem to have had a freer hand in organising their schools, provided they achieved creditable academic results, than they have today.

With the benefit of hindsight, it seems to me that Miss Whyte was near the vanguard of educational thinking. As I have said, the High School was not streamed. We had a School Council. Comparing notes in later life with contemporaries elsewhere, I find that this was unusual in the extreme. There was certainly no School Council in the boys' Grammar School, but at the High School each form elected two representatives, and a form meeting briefed them on points to raise at the termly council meeting, which was presided over by the Head Girl.

She discussed with Miss Whyte the issues raised, reported back to the next council meeting, and the representatives reported back to their forms. I was on more than one occasion in my school life a form representative and valued the honour. Miss Whyte's successor soon put paid to the School Council.

When the 1945 general election was announced, Miss Whyte arranged for each of the three candidates to come and talk to the senior girls. The three sessions took place in school time, so attendance was compulsory. When Miss Whyte decided to retire – I think in the summer of 1945 – she called the senior girls and the staff together one afternoon and told us of her intention. She said that we were her friends, and she wanted us to be the first to know. I think she was quite unusual.

The senior mathematics teacher was Miss Ives, a brilliant teacher if you were mathematically inclined, as I was. In our first year we were introduced to geometry and in our second year to algebra. Beyond that we did not go, unless we wanted to pursue scientific careers, in which case special arrangements were made in the sixth form.

Our science education was scrappy and inadequate, and I think it was typical of what was offered in single-sex girls' grammar/high schools at the time. Girls in mixed-sex schools fared much better. In our second year (Lower IV) we did a year's physics, and in our third year (Upper IV) a year's chemistry. Both courses were taught by Mr Whitney, the Grammar School science master. It seemed daring to be venturing into the shared middle territory between the two schools and actually entering the science labs and having very limited hands-on use of the equipment, but I don't think we gained much from such a cursory introduction.

In our fourth year (Lower V), when preparation for School Certificate began seriously, we started a two-year biology course with a pleasant and popular youngish teacher, Miss Oates, and our exam results were very creditable. In the sixth form High School girls and Grammar School boys who wanted to do science subjects for Higher School Certificate worked together, taught in part by Mr Whitney and in part by Miss Oates.

Girls usually took three years over this course since there was a lot of catching up to do to cover the inadequacies of the earlier years.

In addition to geometry, a new subject to us all, in our first year, we started to learn French, again a new subject for us all. Our teacher was Mrs Huggett. In addition to the usual grind of vocabulary and grammar – dull at that stage – she taught us French songs, presumably to give us the feel of the language. We sang them softly, so as not to disturb neighbouring classrooms. With a good deal of encouragement and a glass or two of wine, I can still render 'Frere Jacques,' 'Au Clair de la Lune,' 'Sur le Pont D'Avignon,' 'En Passant par la Lorraine' and 'Baa, Baa Brebin Noir' – the last her own translation, I think. Not bad after 70 years. She was a good teacher, and we loved her.

Later French teachers were less charismatic, and after the first year it was not one of my favourite subjects, but I got by pretty well.

In our second year (Lower IV) we were introduced to Latin, which I loved from the start. I loved its economy and logical construction and even enjoyed the rhythm of 'Mensa, Mensa, Mensam' and 'Servus, Serve, Servum'. Later I greatly enjoyed the challenge of Latin prose and the flow of Latin verse.

The senior history teacher was Miss Lloyd-Smith, an important influence in my school years. I have no doubt that she was a good socialist – it came through all the time. And she was an internationalist. Although our history syllabus was at core the conventional classical civilisations in the first year, followed by the usual run through English history, she set English history in its wider context. She introduced us to the beginnings of Islam. When we were studying the Reformation in England, she told us about Luther and Calvin and also Ignatius Loyola and the Jesuits. We learned about the European 'benevolent despots' and were introduced sympathetically to the French Revolution.

We knew about the slave trade and the abolitionist movement and, when we were studying Palmerston's foreign policy, she dwelt more than she need have done on the American Civil War. I encountered again Abraham Lincoln, hero of Mr Playford of Gladstone Street. Miss Lloyd-Smith read us the Gettysburg Address. I say she read it – she had the text in front of her – but I think she knew it by heart and recited it. We discussed it in class and, at the end of the lesson, several of us asked if we might borrow the text to make our own copies. I soon had it by heart myself and have it still. Miss Lloyd Smith and Mr Playford lie behind my decision to study history for my degree.

The senior English mistress was Miss Wilkinson. Tiny and fierce, she lived with her mother in one of the villages near Kettering. She was a goat-keeper as well as an English teacher. Notoriously sharp of tongue and short of fuse, you crossed her at your peril.

Miss Wilkinson also was a good socialist – there never was any doubt about that. When those meetings with the parliamentary candidates for the 1945 general election took place, she managed to be one of the supervising teachers for the Labour and Conservative candidates' sessions, and gave John Profumo a very hard time indeed over the Conservatives' between-the-wars record but fed Gilbert Mitchison with helpful leading questions. I was not actually taught by Miss Wilkinson until I entered the sixth form, but I benefited from her English syllabus throughout my school career.

I think the idea was that we should be taught to use the language in as many ways as possible. We had to parse and analyse and spell correctly, of course, and we had to read and understand set texts. The examination system required that.

But we were also introduced early on to debating practice. We learned that you had a proposer and seconder for a motion, an opposer and seconder, that a chairman presided, that the main proponents summed up at the end and that then there was a formal vote. The subjects we chose to debate were probably pretty trivial, but we knew and used the procedure.

When we studied a play, we chose a scene to produce for the other forms in our year. The actors dressed up and learned their parts by heart. I remember playing the wicked Duke Frederick in *As You Like It* in the scene where he discovers that Orlando is the son of Sir Rowland de Boys. I also remember Miss Wilkinson getting very cross when another form was presenting the funeral scene from *Julius Caesar* and the crowd seemed to be too apathetic. "You are furious," she shouted at them. "Your hero has been murdered. You want to go on the rampage. Don't stand there like a crowd of prissy schoolgirls wrapped in sheets!" She got them going in the end.

We had to write formal essays, of course, and to engage in primitive literary criticism, but there was also a lot of free writing, including the writing of poetry.

These were the high points for me: mathematics, Latin, history and English. Geography I continued to find dull and boring. All it seemed to require was a good memory, which I have, and I had no difficulty in achieving good marks, but I did not enjoy the experience. My children and grandchildren have been more fortunate, and I wish I had been able to engage with the kind of geography they studied.

There was a slot in the timetable labeled needlework/domestic science. I remember making a pair of white cotton knickers, an apron to wear for cookery lessons and some rock buns – that's about all. It was not at all like the cosy, relaxed afternoons with Miss Tye at Gladstone Street. At the High School we were required to stitch away in grim silence. Fortunately, at the end of our third year and the beginning of the School Certificate course, someone – not us – decided which of us would study domestic science for School Certificate and who would study Latin. I don't think there was ever any question in my case.

Scripture was on the timetable – it had to be – but it did not seem to be considered an academic subject. I don't remember ever doing any written class work or homework, and there were no end-of-term exams in scripture. It came as quite a surprise to me to discover later on that scripture could be taken as a School Certificate subject and was widely held to be a doddle. I don't think it was taken seriously at Kettering High School.

Gymnastics I enjoyed. I have already described our outdoor activities as young children, and I happily took to all the business with wall bars, parallel bars, vaulting horses, ropes and such. Outdoor ball games were another thing altogether – hockey in particular was absolutely another thing – it did not take me long to realise I was not cut out to be a hockey player. A lot of time seemed to be taken up with practicing various skills: 'dribbling', 'passing, 'bullying', 'shooting' and probably others that I have forgotten. If the business end of a hockey stick was raised above shoulder level, somebody would shout 'sticks' and that gave some sort of advantage to the other side. Just as well. You could suffer quite enough damage from opponents' hockey sticks round your ankles, never mind having them waved about your ears.

When we formed teams and played a match, I quickly discovered the safest place to be was on the forward line – a wing if possible. If you were a back, you were very likely to be tackled and, if you played goal keeper – well, you had to be a martyr or a masochist. If you were out on the extreme edge of the forward line, you could often look busy and engaged without actually getting involved with the ball much at all. My favourite games days were ones when it unequivocally poured with rain and we had to stay in school.

CHAPTER 21
High School occasions

HARDLY AN OCCASION really, but dinner-time at the High School is worth a mention. There were three options: going home or to someone else's home; bringing a packed lunch; or having a school dinner. Nearly all the town girls went home, even though we had only an hour's break during the war years. My friend and classmate Ruth Painter lived on the very edge of Kettering – a good quarter of an hour's ride on her bike – but it would never have occurred to Ruth or her family that she should ever do anything other than go home.

Heather went every day to 'Aunt Marge', an old friend of her mother's who lived in Kettering. It was a complicated business as many of the dinner components were rationed and arrangements had to be made to accommodate this fact, but made they were.

June, Audrey and I obviously could not go home for dinner, so to begin with we took packed lunches – we were deeply suspicious of food cooked by anyone we didn't know. So, food rationing not withstanding, our mothers made sandwiches every morning with whatever was available. However, the school dinners didn't look too bad, not that different from home dinners in fact and were not very expensive, rations were reduced and sandwich fillings became increasingly difficult to find so, what with one thing and another, we took the plunge and signed up for school dinners.

Mrs Brookes, the school cook, was married to Mr Brookes, the caretaker. I don't expect they saw much of each other during the working day, as Mr Brookes's domain was the basement, seeing that the boiler fire was stoked and the heating system working, while Mrs Brookes, of course, was sited in the inappropriately positioned kitchen on the top floor.

Mrs Brookes and her staff had to prepare and serve dinner to the

Grammar School boys and then immediately turn to, clear and set up the dining-room and serve the High School girls. It must have made for a very rushed and stressful couple of hours or so in the middle of the day. The dinners were pretty solid and stodgy – steamed steak and kidney puddings, mince and mash, stews, that kind of thing – followed by milk puddings or steamed puddings or sometimes stewed fruit, but we didn't have to surrender any food coupons or points, so it really helped with the meal planning at home.

The dinner arrangements were quite civilised really – we all stood behind our chairs, and the teacher on dinner duty intoned a formal grace: "For what we are about to receive may we be truly thankful." Then we sat down, and the meal began. There were 11 girls at each table, we more or less kept to the same places throughout the year, and we were mixed age-wise. A senior girl, usually a sixth former, sat at the head of each table and dispensed the main item. She was flanked by two slightly less senior girls who served the accompaniments – vegetables, gravy, custard and such – and the plates were passed down the table.

At first, kitchen staff brought the food to the tables, but I suppose kitchen staff were increasingly difficult to come by, and pretty soon senior girls – Lower and Upper Fifth formers known as 'stewards' – performed this duty on a rota system. I don't remember if the stewards were volunteers or pressed men, but in any case most people quite liked taking their turn. You got a free dinner, usually a very generously proportioned one, for your trouble.

We were supposed to eat everything, but this didn't always happen. Take any collection of 11 schoolgirls, and there will be some picky eaters and some with hollow legs. Generally everything on the table was cleared and no questions asked. If someone chose to eat just potatoes and gravy, all the more for everybody else. The mixed-age tables were quite a good idea: you got to know a few girls from different parts of the school, and often ad hoc advice and support was handed out over the spotted dick and custard. One girl, older than me, whom I got to know at the dinner able, helped me to make an important decision later on – but we shall come to that in due course.

The first major set occasion in the school year was the Christmas Carol Service, a tradition, I think, inherited by Miss Whyte from her predecessor. There were two, or possibly three, performances on consecutive afternoons a week or so before the end of the autumn term. Space in the school hall was at a premium, and you were allowed to invite only one guest, though a small sibling could be brought along and sit on a bench with other little ones in front of the main audience. My mum came every year, and one year, when Auntie Rene and Ann were living with us, Ann came too.

There was a traditional pattern to the carol service, followed every year. We liked it that way. At the beginning, the audience was in place, and the choir, reinforced by some senior girls, was on the corridor-wide balcony that ran down the length of the hall at first-floor level. The school up to and including the Lower Fifth processed in, two by two and form by form, singing O Come All Ye Faithful and took their previously allotted places in the hall. They were followed by the Upper Fifth girls, clad in scarlet cassocks borrowed from various churches, singing Here We Come A-wassailing, and they too took their places.

There were three key theatrically presented set pieces every year. Near the beginning the little girls, eight and nine-year-olds from Form I, gathered round a crib on the platform and sang the 'rocking' carol: "Little Jesus, sweetly sleep, do not stir" etc. Even at the age of 11, I found this slightly squirm inducing, and by the time I was in the Sixth Form I definitely thought it mawkishly sentimental, but it was the only false note for me.

The next set piece was We Three Kings. Three senior girls with good singing voices, gorgeously robed and crowned in Eastern fashion, processed down the central aisle of the hall and onto the stage, bearing their gifts, while the choir sang the first verse and chorus of the carol. The soloists turned to face the audience and each sang her verse:

> Born a King on Bethlehem's plain
> Gold I bring to crown Him again etc

then

> Frankincense to offer have I etc

and

> Myrrh is mine, its bitter perfume
> Breathes of life of gathering gloom etc

each verse followed by a soft rendering of the chorus by the choir. After the last chorus, a crescendo of sound as the whole school joined in a full-throated rendering of the final verse:

> Glorious now behold Him arise
> King and God and sacrifice
> Heaven sings 'Hallelujah'
> 'Hallelujah' the Earth replies.

It was very impressive, as was the last of the set pieces, the Boar's Head carol. A senior girl, clad in a medieval page's garb, again walked up the aisle and onto the platform, carrying aloft with straightened arms, a realistic papier mache boar's head, apple in mouth, on a silver tray garlanded with evergreen. This girl was not required to sing; indeed, she had her work cut out holding that position for the length of the carol for, although the head and tray were light, it was quite a strain, and the bearer was greatly relieved when the last chorus:

> Caput apri defero
> > Reddens laudes domino

died away.

The year we were in the Lower Sixth, my old friend Audrey was chosen to carry the boar's head. She had grown very tall. We had started out more or less the same size at four and a half but, by the time we were 16 or 17, she was at least five inches taller than me. Her ash blonde hair had not darkened as she grew older, and she looked magnificent in the page's costume. I was very proud of her.

The theatrical pieces were interspersed with carols in English, French and Latin and one German carol. German was offered as a subject in the Sixth Form, and the German group always sang Stille Nacht, which I always found very moving. The service ended with a rousing rendering by everyone in the hall of Hark the Herald Angels Sing. There were no Bible readings – unusual in a carol service.

By the end of my schooldays I was convinced that the Christmas story was just that – a story, like the Greek myths. But I always enjoyed the carol service for its familiarity and its drama. In the same way, I can today enjoy an occasional church service as a traditional cultural event. I enjoy the setting, the music, the vestments, the ceremony, even the smells and bells if it's that sort of church, without in the least subscribing to the beliefs at the heart of it.

The other big annual event was Speech Day, aka Prize Day. Individual prizes were awarded only for academic success, measured by the end-of-year in-school examinations or by School Certificate or Higher School Certificate. There were no prizes for effort or attendance or public spirit or anything like that. The prizes were always books. In the lower forms you took what you were given; older girls were allowed to choose their book titles. Whether this had always been school policy or whether it was dictated by wartime shortages and later relaxed when the war ended, I have no idea.

I was awarded a prize every year I was at school. The first one, I remember, was a rather nice edition of *Nicholas Nickleby*. As a senior pupil, one year I chose the complete works of Shelley and, on another occasion, H A Guerber's *The Myths of Greece and Rome*. I think some sports trophies were presented to house captains on Speech Day, but I am not sure – some were certainly presented at end-of-term assemblies by the Headmistress.

A visiting speaker was, of course, invited to speak to the school and guests and to present the prizes. I remember only two speakers. One was Grace Thornton, an alumna of the High School who achieved a distinguished career in the diplomatic service, not in those days an easy road for women. I'm afraid I don't remember her address at all. But I remember clearly Miss Joan Wake, a leading light in the Northamptonshire Historical Society and a family connection in some way of Hereward the Wake, the Saxon rebel so admired by Mr Playford and by us, his ten-year-old pupils at Gladstone Street.

Miss Wake talked about the importance of local history and local historical sources. She offered a prize, to be awarded the following year, for the best collection of local inscriptions made by an individual or group. I was about 13 at the time, and Heather and I decided to have a go. We duly recorded the inscriptions on the Rothwell Market House and on the Jesus Hospital (an alms house for old men) and various other dates and names inscribed on old buildings. My favourite inscriptions, though, were on tombstones, and I liked the ones that eulogised the departed or those written in the first person as a kind of final message or exhortation. This one I particularly liked:

Farewell vain world, I've had enough of thee

And careless am what thou dost think of me.
Thy smiles I count not, nor thy frowns I fear.
My cares are past, my head lies quiet here.
What faults you saw in me take care to shun
And look at home, there's something to be done.

The name on the stone is Elizabeth Frost, it is dated 1773 and is in the Rothwell churchyard.

Heather and I did not win the prize. It was won by the Sherratt sisters: Fay, who was in my year though not in my form, and June, three or four years older. Incidentally, each of the Sherratt sisters was in turn Head Girl.

Even after the competition was over, I retained an interest in tombstones. In the summer of 1946, when I spent some time at Mile End with Grandma Kirby and Uncle Joe, kind Uncle Joe would sometimes take me with him for the ride when he had to make business trips. One day he took me to Monmouth thinking I might like to look at the shops while he went about his affairs. Looking at shops has never been much in my line – give me an old church any day, and I found one in Monmouth and noted this epitaph:

Goodbye my wife and children all.
I yield to the Almighty's call.
My children dear, all love each other
And cherish your afflicted mother.

It was dated 1842, and I didn't record a name; I guess it was illegible.

Another time we went to Newland where, you may remember, Grandpa Kirby took up a butlering post with Sir Charles Palmer after the business in Coleford failed. There is a truly magnificent church, sometimes called 'The Cathedral of the Forest' at Newland,

and in it I found this gem:

> Interred beneath this stone doth lie
> The mirror of true charitie
> His friends', his God's, his countrie's dear
> The poors' supporter far and near,
> He spent his days in rest and quiet
> And never gave himself to riot.
> A virtue strange in those his days
> When it was scorned and vice was praised,
> He lived long and did survive
> Fully the year of seventy five
> And at last expired, his date
> April 7th in 1668

This paragon was Christopher Bond. The riotous living he eschewed must have accompanied the restoration of King Charles II. I don't think there can have been any such carrying on during the Cromwellian Commonwealth which preceded it.

And there is just one more epitaph. I can't remember or imagine what I was doing in Barton Seagrave, a village near Kettering, probably in 1947, but I noted this one down:

> Mother, tend'rest name of love
> O'er which fond remembrance sighs
> May your spirit blest above
> Meet your offspring in the skies

Unfortunately, I did not record a name or date, perhaps someone was urging me to come along – I don't remember.

I am grateful to Miss Joan Wake: she awakened a new interest for me. My tombstone-reading days are over now, though – creaky knees and failing eyesight make it an impossible pleasure.

There were very few school outings in my schooldays – partly because it was wartime, but I think the idea of broadening children's horizons by exposing them to out-of-school experiences was only beginning to take root. I remember three outings, though.

In 1944 or possibly early in 1945 we were taken to see the film *Henry V*. It was on at one of the Kettering cinemas, and a special afternoon showing for schools was arranged. The film was partly funded by the government as a morale booster. In those end-of-the-war years, life seemed a bit dull and grinding, and a dash of patriotism did not come amiss. The film was directed by Laurence Olivier, who also starred in the title role.

I have seen it several times since, and find it a bit too swashbuckling for my adult tastes. I much prefer Kenneth Branagh's quieter, more thoughtful 1989 version. But at the time we thought Olivier's film was wonderful. He was every schoolgirl's pinup, and we gloried in his defiant, dramatic delivery of the exhortations to his army.

There was an extra frisson for us in that Shakespeare makes much of the fact that the battle of Agincourt was fought on 25 October, St Crispin's day, and St Crispin, of course, patron saint of shoemakers, was our local saint. There was a Crispin Street in Rothwell – it crossed Ragsdale Street halfway down – and at the High School we always marked the day at our morning assembly by singing the shoemakers' guild song:

> Oh workers of the old time styled
> The gentle craft of leather.
> Young brothers of the ancient guild
> Stand forth once more together.
> Call out again your long array
> In the old time merry manner.
> Once more on gay Saint Crispin's day
> Bring out your blazoned banner!

In truth, I am not sure if it was an ancient guild song or a more recent invention but, whatever, I am glad we sang it in recognition of Dad, Grandpa, Charlie, Len and Uncle Bob and all the other boot and shoe workers on whom our local economy depended.

We were mindful too of Henry V's promise to his comrades:

> Crispin, Crispian shall ne'er go by
> From this day to the ending of the world
> But we in it shall be remembered.
> We few, we happy few,
> We band of brothers ...

And we followed the guild song with the Agincourt song:

> Our king went forth to Normandie
> With grace and might of chivalrie
> And God for him wrought marv'lously
> Wherefore England may call and cry
> Deo gratias, deo gratias, Anglia rede pro Victoria

I wonder if anyone, anywhere, now marks 25 October.

In 1946, I think, the film *Les Enfants du Paradis* was showing in Kettering, and again a special performance for schools was organised, and we were taken to see it. It tells the story of the tragic, ill fated love affair between Baptiste, a theatre mime, and Claire Reine, an actress. The stars, Arletty, Jean Louis Barrault and Pierre Brasseur and the child actors seemed to me perfect, as did the whole film – restrained, elegant and moving.

I loved it then and have loved it since. I have always been to see it again whenever the opportunity offered. I would go to see it today if it were possible.

In the summer of 1947 an optional trip to Stratford was organised by Miss Wilkinson to see *Romeo and Juliet*. I don't remember who the leading players were but Mercutio was played by a young Paul Scofield, another schoolgirl heart-throb. It was my first experience of professional theatre. I had seen plenty of amateur productions – some good, some pretty grim – but this was the real thing, and we loved it. The whole experience – the theatre, the town, our riverside picnic – was magical.

One other visit sticks in my mind, an informal one. When we were in the Lower Sixth, a group of about half a dozen of us decided we would like to visit Cambridge for a day at half term. We asked Miss Lloyd-Smith for her advice. She was a native daughter of Cambridge as well as a graduate of Girton, and she asked if we would like her to meet us and show us around. Indeed we would! And she did us proud, even standing us a restaurant lunch.

We were over-awed by the colleges and enchanted by the walk along the Backs. In the courtyard of Trinity College, we saw an elderly gentleman *walking on the grass*, an expressly forbidden activity! "That," said Miss Lloyd-Smith, "is George Macaulay Trevelyan. The dons are allowed to walk on the grass. It is one of their privileges." George Macaulay Trevelyan! Master of Trinity College! Author of the recently published *English Social History*, which was in our school library! We had never seen a real live don before, nor a real live published author. We stared and we marvelled.

An event that never happened at Kettering High School – or for that matter, I think, at other schools – was a parents' meeting. In fact contact between school and home was minimal, and I don't think this was down to its being wartime. I think it was the norm until perhaps the 1960s. We took home a school report at the end of each term, a single sheet of paper with the school subjects listed on the left and spaces on the right for the teachers to comment – usually a laconic one-liner, even a one-worder; 'good' or 'fair' or 'poor' seemed to be quite acceptable.

There was a space for exam marks and position to be recorded, space for a form teacher's brief comment and that was it. At the last morning assembly of each term, Miss Whyte solemnly reminded us that our reports were addressed to our parents – we had ourselves addressed the envelopes some days previously – and that they should be conveyed intact. We were merely the postmen.

The last day of term we were always dismissed at dinner-time and filed down, form by form, in alphabetical order to receive our reports from Miss Whyte herself. Most of us then opened them as soon as we were out of sight and sound of school.

Any decisions that needed to be taken, like Higher School Certificate subjects, for instance, were taken in school and conveyed home by word of mouth. I expect parents could have objected had they wished to do so. Mine didn't; they happily accepted what I wanted to do. Invitations to the Carol Service and Speech Day were also conveyed by word of mouth. We were given the relevant information in school and told our form teacher if a parent wanted to attend. My mum conscientiously came to seven Carol Services and seven Speech Days, but I don't think she ever came to the school for anything else.

Of course, means of communication were limited in those days in a way that is difficult to envisage in the 21st century. Our school report forms were printed by a commercial printer, as were notifications of school medical examinations, but there were no means of running off a one-off written communication to all parents.

A typist could produce three, or at the most four, carbon copies, and the last one would be pretty dodgy, even if the carbon paper was new. The school had no Roneo duplicator, and photocopiers were, of course, unimaginable. Our internal examination papers were produced on something called, I think, a 'jelly bed', from which copies could be rolled off, one by one. Reading the exam paper, never mind answering the questions, was often quite a challenge.

Also taking into account a shortage of paper, lack of telephones, a school community scattered over a wide area and a wartime bus service that ceased operating at 9pm, it is not perhaps surprising that there was little home/school contact. What a contrast though with the London comprehensives I experienced as a parent and a teacher in the 1960s,'70s and '80s, with our cheque-book style reports, our parents' meetings with individual discussions available on the progress of each child in each subject, and our careful working out with parents and pupil of the most suitable exam course.

CHAPTER 22

The Sixth Form

AT THE END of the summer term 1946, I and my class mates took the Oxford School Certificate examination. I achieved the Very Good grade in mathematics, English literature, Latin, French, biology, history and geography and the Credit grade in English language and art. I was therefore eligible to enter the Sixth Form and could have chosen one of several subject combinations.

At that time, the local newspaper the *Kettering Evening Telegraph* published a full list of examination results, and a day or two later I met Mr Briers in the town. For the second time in my life, he shook my hand. "You're a good girl," he said. "You've always been a good girl." 'Good girl' or 'good boy' was as far as Mr Briers ever went. He didn't do hyperbole.

Traditionally, the Headmistress was form mistress to the Sixth Form. Miss Whyte had retired at the end of the 1945 summer term, and her successor was Miss Woodrow, a modern linguist who had held a senior post at Clifton High School.

The idea behind the form-mistressing was, I'm sure, that the Head should get to know her senior girls in order to advise about careers and courses and other life choices. The administrative aspects of a form mistress's responsibilities, such as registration, dinner money etc, were now taken over by various members of the form.

Miss Woodrow spent time with us discussing school matters and wider, beyond school issues. During her headship relations with the boys' Grammar School were relaxed somewhat. The old head of the Grammar School, Dr Scott, had retired before Miss Whyte and had been succeeded by a Mr Scott (no relation). With the arrival of Miss Woodrow some carefully supervised joint activities took place: a Sixth Form Christmas party, some shared expeditions, even an exchange visit to Holland in the summer of 1947, and no one made a fuss if boys and girls sometimes met at the school gates.

In this more liberal atmosphere, I met and paired up with my first boy friend, but more of David later.

Our first business as Sixth Formers was deciding on our Higher School Certificate courses. To be awarded a University of Oxford Higher School Certificate, you needed at least a 'pass' grade in three principal subjects or in two principal subjects and two subsidiaries. Above the 'pass' standard, you could be awarded a 'good' or a 'very good' and you could also take a separate, more difficult 'distinction' paper.

I think about 20 of the 93 girls who had entered the High School in September 1941 made it into the Sixth Form. We were the Lower Sixth, and there was of course an Upper Sixth – girls from the year above us. We shared a form room with the Upper Sixth for registration, dinner money etc and we had some joint activities and school responsibilities, but in the main we were taught separately.

All of us were studying for the Higher School Certificate; there was no other course available. And most of us were aiming for either university or teacher training college, though two girls went on to a secretarial college and two or three went straight into employment.

I wanted to study history, Latin, English and maths. Not on! Maths was firmly embedded in the science course, which was a shared course with the Grammar School and was geared to the Grammar School timetable. Reluctantly I had to drop maths and settle for subsidiary French instead. The other three I took as principal subjects, and I decided to have a go at the distinction paper in history, something strongly advocated by Miss Lloyd-Smith, who of course taught the history group.

Sadly for us, she was appointed to a senior post at Bedford High School at the end of our Lower Sixth year and was replaced by a very capable new young graduate.

I have already described, in Chapter 20, Miss Wilkinson, the senior English mistress. Now, for the first time in my High School life, I was taught by her. She was a brilliant teacher with a passion for the Romantic poets, whose political philosophy she shared. I developed a similar life-long love of the Romantics, Keats and Shelley in particular.

I loved Keats's condemnation of early capitalism in *Isabella*:

> With her two brothers this fair lady dwelt,
> Enriched from ancestral merchandise,
> And for them many a weary hand did swelt
> In torched mines or noisy factories,
> And many once proud-quiver'd loins did melt
> In blood from stinging whip; with hollow eyes
> Many all day in dazzling river stood,
> To take the rich-ored driftings of the flood.
>
> For them the Ceylon diver held his breath,
> And went all naked to the hungry shark;
> For them his ears gush'd blood; for them in death
> The seal on the cold ice with piteous bark
> Lay full of darts; for them alone did seethe
> A thousand men in troubles wide and dark:
> Half-ignorant, they turn'd an easy wheel,
> That set sharp racks at work, to pinch and peel.

And Shelley's call to revolution from *You Have Nothing To Lose But Your Chains*:

> Men of England, Heirs of Glory,
> Heroes of unwritten story,
> Nurslings of one mighty mother,

Hopes of her, and one another!
Shake your chains to earth like dew
Which in sleep had fallen on you.
Ye are many, they are few.

Miss Wilkinson enjoyed my enjoyment.

The senior Latin mistress was Miss Mitchell, who had been my form teacher in my first year. By 1946 Miss Mitchell was a very ill lady and before the end of our Lower Sixth year she had to withdraw from all her school commitments, though it was said she would return when she was better. In the meantime there was a problem. It was possible to shift around and bring in extra help for lower-school Latin, but Higher School Certificate principal subject Latin was a different matter.

A knight in shining armour rode to our rescue in the unlikely person of Mr W C C Cooke, one of the school governors. I think he must have been about 70 years old at the time. Mr Cooke, retired headmaster of Northampton Boys' Grammar School, classical scholar, poet, life-long bachelor, had served in Flanders during the first world war and sustained a serious wound to his right hand which resulted in the most execrable handwriting I have ever seen and, believe me, I have seen some.

Mr Cooke had never taught girls before, and I'm sure he came forward out of a strong sense of duty, but I'm equally sure that he soon began to relish the experience. He was an excellent teacher, and we were a bright, highly motivated group of four perky and opinionated girls. He was interested in us as people and in the minutiae of our lives. Sometimes he asked Miss Woodrow if he could take us out for coffee in the town if it didn't interfere with anything else we should be doing, and we all enjoyed these little expeditions.

At Christmas he gave us each a little book of his collected poems, written when he was a very young man. It is a charming little memento of a charming old gentleman. Two or three times he agreed to spend time with the whole Sixth Form on 'Classical Studies' – a glance at the culture of Greece and Rome.

After I left school, he invited me out to lunch during the Christmas or Easter vacation of my first university year. After lunch, perhaps emboldened by the glass of wine he had bought me, saying my goodbyes and thank yous, I gave him a chaste, granddaughterly peck on the cheek. A few days later, I received this note in the post:

> Betty kissed me. Yes she did
> When I had helped her put her coat on
> Jealous youth could not forbid
> I was left with this to gloat on
> Say I'm getting old and grey
> Say good luck has often missed me
> *Virides* note this I pray
> Betty kissed me.

Virides was an in-joke. My friend and fellow student Fay had once, in the course of a Latin Unseen or Prose, confused *virides* (green ones) with *viriles* (strong men). Mr Cooke found this hilarious and always referred to our boy friends as *virides*. "How were the *virides* this weekend, then?," he would ask on a Monday morning. Or "Any new *virides* on the horizon?" at the beginning of a new term. Sadly, he died quite suddenly. I shall always remember him with great affection.

And talking of boy friends, David Godfrey and I got chatting at one of the joint activities that were permitted by Miss Woodrow and Mr Scott – probably the 1946 Christmas party, but I don't really remember. We danced together, inexpertly, but found that we got on quite well and saw a fair amount of each other during the next 18 months. David was also in his Lower Sixth year, studying science subjects for Higher School Certificate, aiming to do a medical degree, which I believe he ultimately did.

David's father, C W Godfrey, was the geography master at the Grammar School, enormously popular with his pupils. His mother was a junior school teacher who had been able to go back to work when wartime exigencies permitted the employment of married women teachers. Blessedly for her, as she loved the work and was not mad about domesticity.

David was the youngest of the family. His sister, Margaret, was a year ahead of me at the High School, and his brother, Michael, was, I think, doing military service. The Godfrey household, like the Andrew one, was a socialist stronghold. Mr Godfrey in later years became a Labour mayor of Kettering, and David was a member of the Labour League of Youth. I wasn't. As I have already said, Mum and I were increasingly uneasy about the Labour government's foreign policy. Still, David and I often went to Labour League of Youth socials, innocent, alcohol-free affairs which took place in the full glare of the electric lights of the school hall hired for the occasion.

We occasionally went to the cinema and cuddled in the back row, but we hadn't much money and spent a lot of our time together in each other's homes.

David was a keen jazz fan and played the clarinet. A group of us often listened to jazz records, and David and another boy who played the trumpet would play along. I quite liked the music but never became a keen fan. Mr Godfrey enjoyed classical orchestral music and, if there was a concert on the wireless in the living room, he would sit on a dining chair facing the wireless from a distance of about two feet, conducting energetically with both arms. If you wanted to go through the living room to the kitchen beyond, you had to open and shut the doors very quietly and walk on tiptoe.

Sometimes there was a jazz session in the front room and an orchestral concert in the living room at the same time.

At our home David was intrigued by toddler John. He had no experience of small children and enjoyed playing with him. David once had the bright idea that we would make John a chocolate Easter egg, using two egg cups as moulds, then sticking the two bits of moulded chocolate together with melted chocolate to make an egg shape. Sweets were still rationed although the war was over, but I rarely bought my sweet ration unless I was giving someone sweets or chocolate as a present, so we were able to buy the requisite chocolate.

It didn't work. When the chocolate set, we couldn't get it out of the moulds, so we melted it again and made chocolate drops instead. It was a lot of fun, but messy.

David's and my relationship did not survive my departure for university. He was staying on for a third year in the Sixth Form, and by Christmas we both had new partners.

CHAPTER 23
Moving on

By the time I was in the Sixth Form, I was quite clear that I wanted to go to university and do a history degree. My family and teachers were supportive, and that was what we worked towards. Miss Lloyd Smith was keen for me to apply to Girton, her own Alma Mater, and I was quite happy to give it a go.

There were two stages to the entry process. First, a written paper, for which you or, in most cases, your school made the arrangements. Some candidates were weeded out at this stage, but those whose written paper was acceptable were called for a one-to-one interview at Girton.

The date of the written paper was fixed for the day on which the then Princess Elizabeth married Philip Mountbatten, a public holiday unless you happened to be taking the Girton entrance paper. I did the paper in the dining-room of Miss Woodrow's apartment at Hillside. Miss Woodrow and her mum, who was staying with her at the time, took turns watching over me, interspersed, I think, with sessions listening to the wireless commentary on the wedding. They supplied me with coffee and an excellent sponge cake made by Mrs Woodrow.

The paper, as far as I remember, comprised exercises in logical thinking and deduction rather than reproduction of factual information.

A few weeks later, I received a letter telling me I had passed the written paper and should attend Girton College for an interview on a specified day a week or so before Christmas 1947.

I honestly remember very little about the interview except that it was conducted by a lady don, probably in her 50s, who sat on the floor and invited me to do likewise. I, of course, did as I was asked, but was completely nonplussed. Grown-up women in my world didn't sit on floors. I couldn't imagine Miss Woodrow doing any such thing. Floors were hard and draughty places, suitable for cats and rabbits and toddler games but not for anyone who had the option of a chair, and there were several comfortable looking ones in the room. Maybe it was a test of my sang-froid. If so, I failed it and was not offered a place at Girton.

In those days, and indeed for many years afterwards, it was not unusual for Oxbridge hopefuls to spend a third year in the Sixth Form, concentrating on entry to the college of their choice after their Higher School Certificate was behind them. This option was mooted by Miss Woodrow and my other teachers, but I was not keen on kicking my heels for a year when my friends and contemporaries had moved on. And, truth to tell, I had been a bit underwhelmed by the Girton experience.

University application was a much more casual and haphazard business in the 1940s than it is today. There was no central organisation or clearing system as there is now. You just took advice from anyone with advice to give, made your own investigations and waited for your Higher School Certificate results before making your application.

I considered Leicester (then a university college, becoming a full university in 1957) and Nottingham (a full university from 1948), both easily accessible from home. Manchester was mentioned by one of my teachers, and there was Bristol. I had been to Bristol once when staying with the family in the Forest. Auntie Emmie, one of Mum's half-sisters lived there, so Bristol was on the list.

One day in the spring or early summer of 1948 I was in Kettering on my way to meet David when I met Barbara, who was two or three years older than me. We had sat on the same school dinner table one year, when she had been one of the big girls dishing out the vegetables and custard and I had been one of the smaller fry receiving them, but we had developed an amicable relationship and always stopped to chat when we met.

On this occasion we exchanged news for a few minutes: Barbara told me she was an undergraduate reading modern languages at Bristol and was thoroughly enjoying life there. She was very excited when I said I was considering Bristol and invited me to tea a day or two later so that she could tell me more.

At Barbara's house I tried on her Bristol scarf, an austerity version in those days but quite elegant: a length of black woven woolen material with maroon and white fringes at each end and a Bristol University badge appliquéd above the fringe. It cost two or three clothing coupons according to length and a sum of money that I don't remember. Barbara also let me look at her University of Bristol Union Diary, which gave details of all the societies and clubs that students were eligible to join, including a Student Branch of the Communist Party!

Now that was something I was interested in. In my ignorance and innocence I did not realise that in those heady post-war days every decent students union boasted a plethora of political and inter-national societies. The universities and colleges were full of young people whose education had been interrupted by the war and now, returning victorious from the fight against fascism, were able to resume their studies thanks to the government's Further Education and Training Scheme. They had every intention of having a say in where the post-war world was going, and who had a better right to do so?

Bristol was by no means unique in the opportunities it offered, but I didn't know that then and decided firmly that that was where I wanted to go.

The Higher School Certificate results came out somewhere around the middle of August, and I had a distinction in history, goods in English and Latin and a pass in subsidiary French – an adequate qualification for acceptance by the history department at Bristol University and, equally importantly, for a county major scholarship of £180 a year. It sounds a paltry sum now but it covered my fees and living expenses in term time. Like most other students I got holiday jobs but I don't remember anybody who had to get a job in term time to make ends meet.

So there I was one day at the end of September 1948, eager and anxious in equal measure, arriving at the Students Union building for the Freshers' Squash, an event for new first-year undergraduates where all the student societies displayed their wares and looked for recruits. There was a tall, slender rather good looking young man on the steps selling the *Daily Worker*, the newspaper of the Communist Party of Great Britain and precursor of the *Morning Star*. I bought a copy. The young man was called Chris Birch. But that's the beginning of another story, one that ran and ran for more than 60 years and is running still. Maybe I'll write it for you one day.

INDEX